Dirty W

Dirty Water

JUDITH COOK

UNWIN
PAPERBACKS

LONDON SYDNEY WELLINGTON

First published in Great Britain by the Trade Division of Unwin
Hyman Limited, 1989

UNWIN HYMAN LIMITED
15–17 Broadwick Street
London W1V 1FP

Allen & Unwin Australia Pty Ltd
8 Napier Street, North Sydney, NSW 2060, Australia

Allen & Unwin New Zealand Pty Ltd with the Port Nicholson Press
Compusales Building, 75 Ghuznee Street, Wellington, New Zealand.

British Library Cataloguing in Publication Data

Cook, Judith, *1933–*
    Dirty water.
1. Great Britain. Water supply industries
I. Title
338.4′76281′0941
ISBN 0–04–440546–4

Phototypeset by Input Typesetting Ltd, London
Printed in Great Britain by Cox & Wyman Ltd, Reading

This book is dedicated to my grandchildren,
Daniel, Joshua and Sam
in the fervent hope that we might try to
leave them a cleaner world

Contents

It is difficult and indeed almost impossible to reconcile
the rights and interests of the public with the claims
of an individual company seeking as its natural and
legitimate object, the largest private gain.

Joseph Chamberlain

... government is nothing more than a national
association acting on the principles of society

Tom Paine, *The Rights of Man*

There is no such thing as society, only individuals.

Margaret Thatcher

Acknowledgements

First and foremost, Alan Jackson of the National and Local Government Officers Association (NALGO) for all the research material provided by the Water Department of that union. Also Greenpeace, especially Tim Birch whose report, *Poison in the System*, should be required reading for all interested in the subject of water pollution. Thanks – yet again – to Friends of the Earth. Other people who helped a great deal include Anne Taylor MP and Janey Buchan MEP. I have had to draw on a great deal of material to put this book together and so far as possible I have credited it. If there have been any lapses then please take this as an acknowledgement for all the material used.

Glossary

I have spelled out the various acronyms when they have been used for the first time but, as a further guideline, I also give them below.

CIA   Chemical Industries Association
COD   Chemical Oxygen Demand
COPA   Control of Pollution Act 1974
DoE   Department of the Environment
EC   European Commission. (When quoting directly I have found some authorities use the term 'EEC' so I have used it in those circumstances.)
HMIP   Inspectorate of Pollution
MAFF   Ministry of Agriculture, Fisheries and Food
NRA   National Rivers Authority
RQO   River Quality Objective
USEPA   United States Environmental Protection Agency
WRC   Water Research Council
WSPLCs   Water Service Public Limited Companies

PART I

The State of Our Water

1

'. . . the rights and interests of the public'

It is not fortuitous that water plays such a large part in classical imagery and that of the Bible. Along with bread, it is the essential for life itself; man cannot live without it. From prehistoric times wells were sacred, places of worship, places where local deities had to be placated. It is thought that in northern Europe heads were thrown into them as an offering, for skulls have been found in ancient wells.

Classical Greece and ancient Rome absorbed earlier beliefs, and lesser gods, water nymphs and other such deities were considered as being in charge of wells, water courses, streams and rivers. Desert heavens, whether in the Koran or *A Thousand and One Nights*, contain abundant water and for the Moors who built the great palace of the Alhambra in Granada, the utmost luxury was to channel water down from the mountains into the magnificent gardens and there use it to form pools, water courses and artificial streams.

Not only does man need water to survive, he requires a clean and reliable supply of it – something which has, at least, been accepted since the latter half of the nineteenth century in this country. The majority of us have become accustomed to having it always there on tap to use for drinking, cooking, washing and flushing the lavatory. Until recently, the rate we paid for this service was relatively low for it was considered as an essential for a decent and civilised society.

Moreover, for years we bragged about the purity of our drinking water, for were we not continually told that when travelling on the Continent we must *never* drink their water as it could not be trusted? Now all that has changed. As we shall see later, it is not French or German water that is unfit to drink, it is *our* tap water which is suspect. It is *our* rivers, lakes and ground water which are filthy and polluted.

Richard II is remembered in history for successfully quelling the Peasants' Revolt while only a young lad and then going, as it were, downhill all the way until he was deposed by the tough Henry IV. In Shakespeare's play he is an arrogant idler but also a dreamer, given to musing on the ephemeral nature of kingship and dissolving into tears when fate goes against him. But at least historically he appears to have involved himself in one basic public health measure. In 1388, he outlawed the throwing of dung, filth and garbage into ditches or rivers near cities.

However, he does not appear to have succeeded in the long term. Before the days when our own unmaintained sewers burst and flooded houses with crude sewage, we used to laugh at the quaint old ways of the Elizabethans as, to merry shouts of 'Gardez loo!' they emptied their chamber pots and night soil out of their windows into the open ditches or channels that ran down the centre of their streets. (To return to Shakespeare, one of the earliest records of the Shakespeare family in Stratford is a court report of the fining of Will Shakespeare's father for making a midden outside his house . . .)

Those living in London were quite used to taking dirty slops down to the Thames in a wooden bucket, emptying it into the river and then refilling it again for household use.

The poet and playwright Ben Jonson wrote a graphic description of the trip he made along the River Fleet, which had become a sewer. It is worth quoting some of it here as it has uncanny resonances with what is happening in some of our rivers today. Jonson details all the horrid things that find their way into the Fleet (some details of which are best omitted), including:

things that are precipitated down the jakes,
And after swim abroad in ample flakes,
Or that there lay heaped like a usurer's mass,
All was to them the same, they were to pass,
And so they did from Styx to Acheron,
The ever-boiling flood; whose banks upon
Your Fleet Lane Furies, and hot cooks do dwell
That with still-scalding steams make the place Hell.
The sinks run grease, and hair of meazled hogs,
The head, houghs, entrails, and hides of dogs,
For to say truth, what scullion is so nasty,
To put the skins and offal in a pasty?

Three hundred years later things in the inner cities had not
improved a great deal although the water closet had replaced
the jakes for those who were better off. Cholera and typhoid
were, however, regular visitors.

When we are exhorted to look back with favour on Victorian
values there are two sides to that coin – the appallingly insanitary
conditions in which large numbers of working people had to live
and the work of those philanthropists who sought to ameliorate
it.

One mid-nineteenth-century report describes how

every room in these reeking tenements houses a family, often
two. In one cellar a sanitary inspector reports finding a father,
mother, three children and four pigs. In another room an inspector found a man ill with small pox, his wife just recovered from
her eighth confinement, and the children running about half
naked and covered in dirt. Here are seven people living in one
underground kitchen, and a little dead child lying in the same
room. Elsewhere is a poor widow, her three children, and a child
who had been dead for thirteen days.

Needless to say, there was no convenient supply of water available to these families.

As late as 1902, in *People from the Abyss*, Jack London described
those unfortunate enough to end up in the workhouse having to
take baths in pairs. 'Twenty-two men washed in the same tub

of water, including a man whose back was a mass of blood from attacks of vermin and retaliatory scratching.'

It took successive waves of cholera, coupled with hot summers when the Thames ran stinking past the Houses of Parliament, for it to begin to be recognised that a clean and decent water supply and proper sewers were a necessity, not a luxury.

One of the pioneers in the field of clean water and health was Dr John Snow, famous for his closure of the Broad Street pump. An epidemic of cholera had occurred around the Broad Street area of central London and Dr Snow discovered that almost all the victims had one thing in common – they had drawn their water at a certain pump in Broad Street. He immediately had it closed down and the epidemic began to subside almost at once.

In view of the discussions taking place today, it is interesting to note what Dr Richard Bates said in a paper, in 1979, called 'Environmental Health Perspectives':

One can imagine the reaction which might occur today if it were proposed to close down the Broad Street pump on evidence of the kind obtained by John Snow.

Many scientists would point out that it had not been demonstrated conclusively that the water was the cause of the disease. They would be troubled because of the lack of satisfactory theoretical knowledge to explain how the water caused the disease. Furthermore, other habits of those who became ill had not been adequately investigated, so it would not be possible to rule out other causes of the disease. The scientists would have been correct. Others would have pointed out that some members of the community who drank at the Broad Street well had not succumbed to cholera. Thus, even if there were something wrong with the water there must be other factors involved, and if we could control these we would not have to be concerned about the water. These conclusions are also correct. Some who consumed water from the Broad Street well would have objected to closing it because the taste of water from other wells was not as agreeable. Finally, if the pump had been owned by an individual who sold the water, he would certainly have protested against closing down his business on the basis of inconclusive evidence of hazard. Meanwhile, of course, people would have gone on dying.

In 1848, the first Public Health Act was enacted which established Sanitary Authorities and authorised the setting up of local health boards with the power to supply water for their area, providing no private companies were already doing it. This was obviously insufficient for in 1865–6 a Royal Commission was set up to look into the state of the nation's water.

It discovered that much of the water being supplied to the public was of inadequate quality or downright impure. Between the years 1873 and 1876 when Joseph Chamberlain was Mayor of Birmingham, he set about ensuring a decent supply of water to the city, coupled with improved sanitation. Birmingham at that time was serviced by a private water company and in 1874 a parliamentary commission into river pollution discovered that this company provided unfiltered river water containing 'a very large proportion of actual organic matter of unmistakable animal origin'. In fact they drew their water from a stream heavily polluted with sewage and manufacturing refuse and supplied it just as it was straight to the consumer.

Further Public Health Acts were introduced in 1872 and 1875, the latter by Disraeli which put public health at the forefront of state responsibilities, making it incumbent on public authorities to see that every dwelling house had an adequate supply of wholesome water within reasonable distance. However, these authorities were still specifically excluded from taking action that might affect the commercial interests of existing private water companies.

In 1876, the Rivers Pollution Prevention Act was passed which had limited powers to stop the kind of pollution which had brought about the cholera epidemics in the 1860s and 1870s, although it was not very effective. It also stated that while the local authority was bound to dispose of ordinary sewage matter, together with liquid discharges from factories, no injurious matter 'like chemical refuse or steam may be drained or let off into a sewer'.

Gradually, throughout the 1870s, these and other reforms did lead to a vast increase in municipal ownership and a dramatic improvement in the quality of water supplied. As the National Association of Local Government Officers (NALGO) says in its publication, *Water Down the Drain?*: 'the private water companies found there was no money in public health and displayed little imagination in their response to the challenges confronting them. Providing a comprehensive service rarely paid much profit, so private companies did not do it; anticipating rising demand was not as attractive to them as supplying extra water where and when it was needed so they stuck to a "follow the market" policy.'

In 1930, the Land Drainage Act came into force which established local drainage boards based on catchment areas for water rather than local authority boundaries, and in 1937 the government set up the Central Advisory Water Committee to advise on a national policy. Their findings influenced the new 1945 Water Act which led to the amalgamation of water supply undertakings. Between 1945 and 1974, the total number of undertakings fell from 1,186 to 157 including some 28 private companies.

In 1973, the then Conservative government brought in a new Water Act which established the present structure of the industry with ten new Water Authorities – Anglian, North West, Northumbrian, Severn Trent, South West, Southern, Thames, Welsh, Wessex and Yorkshire and these took over the responsibilities of the 157 undertakings plus 29 river authorities and 1,393 sewage disposal authorities. About 20 per cent of water supplied is still provided by the 28 private water companies.

Providing a clean public water supply had as big, if not bigger, effect on public health than all the breakthroughs in new drugs. It virtually wiped out typhoid and cholera, dysentery, hepatitis, and gastro-enteritis became much more rare – although the current state of our water has led to a significant increase in some of these latter diseases.

It was left to Margaret Thatcher's reforming zeal to change all that and to prepare us to make a smart leap backwards into the nineteenth century. Water, that stuff which falls from heaven and rises unbidden from the ground, should not be ours of right. We should have to pay for it and it offers those totally oriented towards market forces the ultimate privatisation – apart from the air we breathe. Water must become profitable. People who are already wealthy and can afford to invest in it can become even wealthier by becoming shareholders in the one substance we cannot possibly do without.

As we prepare to make this giant leap backwards, let us reflect on what Joseph Chamberlain said back in 1894 with regard to water: 'It is difficult and indeed almost impossible to reconcile *the rights and interests of the public* with the claims of an individual company seeking as its material and legitimate object the largest private gain' (my emphasis).

2

Into Europe

When considering the state of water in the UK, which is essential to the subject matter of the book, reference will need to be made to the European Commission and EEC Regulations, Directives and Standards. So it is necessary to look at the background to these. I am indebted for much of the information in this chapter to the water department of NALGO and to a paper presented to the European Parliament by Ken Collins MEP and David J. Earnshaw, the latter being a lecturer in European Politics at Hatfield Polytechnic and a researcher for Ken Collins on this subject.

After considering a memorandum on the environment which had been submitted to it, the European Commission decided in 1972, at a meeting of Heads of State, that in future 'particular attention will be given to intangible values and to protecting the environment' in EEC policy-making, and in November of the following year the EEC adopted the Community's First Action Programme on the Environment.

This covered four fields – reduction, elimination and prevention of pollution; the non-damaging use and rational management of land, environment and natural resources; general action to protect the environment; and international cooperation on it. The result of this policy has been the adoption of 120 Directives, decisions and regulations of which just under a quarter relate directly to water. The legislation set common standards for environmental quality, for emissions and for treatment procedures such as waste storage and disposal.

There are four main forms of EEC legislation. Article 189 of the Treaty of Rome sets them out. They are: Regulations – which are of general application, binding in their entirety and directly applicable to all Member States; Directives – binding on each Member State as to the result to be achieved but national authorities choose form and method; Decisions – binding in their entirety on those they address; and Recommendations and Opinions – which have no binding force.

However, with regard to the environment, many problems remained until the amendment of the various treaties into the Single European Act of 1987 which was signed – let it be noted – by the present government. Article 100A(3) of this Act states that: 'The Commission, in its proposals laid down in paragraph 1 concerning health, safety, environmental protection and consumer protection, will take as a base a high level of protection.' At the time of writing, there are eighteen Decisions, fourteen Directives and three Resolutions on water in force with further Directives in the pipeline. Britain has been notable for years for fighting Directives on pollution, dragging its feet on implementing them and trying to find ways around them. This could cost it dear in the run up to privatisation for there are whole areas regarding such things as lead and nitrates in water which could hold the whole deal up.

EEC Directives impose four different kinds of obligations on Member States – the need to adapt national legislation, administrative structures and procedures so that they conform to the rules and procedures set out in the Directive; the need to put these rules and procedures into practice; the need to ensure that the quality of the environment meets the standards or the ends set out in the Directive; and the fourth concerns communications that Member States must make to the Commission to exercise control over the other three obligations. Article 169 of the Rome Treaty states:

If the Commission considers that a Member State has failed to fulfil an obligation under this Treaty, it shall deliver a reasoned opinion on the matter after giving the State concerned the opportunity to submit its observations. If the State concerned does not comply with the opinion within the period laid down by the Commission, the latter may bring the matter before the Court of Justices.

In June 1987, Commissioner Stanley Clinton Davis informed our Parliament that no less than twenty-two proceedings for infringement of environmental legislation were pending against the UK. Eleven of these relate to Water Directives. The majority have been brought due to failings in practical implementation. The remainder concern instances of incomplete implementation. The proceedings range from polluted bathing water to nitrates and lead in drinking water.

According to the paper by Ken Collins and David Earnshaw, the Council Directive of 15 July 1980, relating to the quality of drinking water intended for human consumption (80/778/EEC), can be regarded as the 'cornerstone' of EEC environmental policy. The Directive requires Member States to ensure that by July 1985 drinking water meets certain values for a list of sixty-two parameters. Derogations, that is, exclusions, from the provisions of that Directive are allowed only to take account of situations arising from the nature and structure of the ground in the area from which the supply in question emanates and situations arising from exceptional meteorological conditions. Maximum Admissible Concentrations (MACs) – fixed in the Directive – may be exceeded in the event of emergencies for a limited time, only if there is no risk to health and water cannot be supplied in any other way. Until 1985, under Article 20 Member States could 'in exceptional cases and for geographically defined population groups' request that the Commission permit delays in complying with the MACs, but only where an improvement programme with an appropriate timetable is established. This provision has now expired.

When the Directive was adopted, only Denmark could comply with it, as it happened to coincide anyway with the adoption of legislation in that country regulating the quality of its drinking water. Other countries ran into difficulties. By the end of the two years in which measures should have been taken to incorporate the measures into national law, not a single Member State had communicated to the Commission what it intended doing to comply with the Directive. Legal transposition of the Directive was, therefore, held up for four years.

In August 1987, the Commission initiated proceedings against Belgium, France, Germany and Ireland for failure to implement the Directive fully. The UK received notification a little later that it had failed to satisfy the Commission that it had implemented the Directive as it applies to private water supplies. Circulars implementing the Directive apply only to public bodies responsible for water supplies.

Article 12 of the Directive states that Member States must ensure regular monitoring of water quality. In December 1987, the Secretary of State for the Environment announced that the UK would, henceforth, interpret the term 'maximum admissible concentration' as applying to individual samples and not to averages over a period. There is a dearth of information as to how other countries actually do monitor their water samples and there is no requirement in the Directive for them to provide this. Obviously, such information would be very useful.

Where Britain could run into real difficulties with the European Commission over privatisation and its water standards are in the parameters regarding nitrates, pesticides and lead, all of which will be dealt with in much more detail later on. According to the authors of this paper, water industry sources have been reported as estimating additional spending needed to comply with the Directive with regard to these pollutants as running into 'several billion pounds'.

Another important Council Directive of 8 December 1975 concerns the quality of bathing water. Directive 76/160 defines bathing water as fresh or sea water in which bathing is explicitly undertaken and is traditionally practised by a large number of bathers. Members are required to set values for a number of parameters according to various standards and guidelines. These values were supposed to have been met by 1985 but, again, derogations may be granted on the basis of management plans being prepared for the water in question. Member States were to submit to the Commission comprehensive reports on their bathing waters.

The Directive was supposed to be incorporated into national legislation by December 1977 but in fact the transposition took between two and eight years with only one Member State complying in 1977. Belgium, the Netherlands and Italy were condemned by the Court of Justices for failure to comply with the Directive, while an infringement procedure was started against the UK following which it responded satisfactorily to the Commission.

By February 1988, Belgium had not adopted all the Directive's procedures, Italy had introduced a number of exceptions for certain parameters, and in the UK there remains doubt about the implementation of the Directive by the means merely of an administrative circular. There are great divergences between the values set by different Member States with regard to the parameters and even greater differences as to what constitutes bathing water. Each Member State applies different criteria to determine bathing areas – monitoring points, kilometres, and so on.

The UK made a complete fool of itself with the tiny number of bathing areas officially designated. Its position was obviously untenable in view of the fact that it originally designated fewer bathing areas than landlocked Luxemburg, and the Commission expressed its dissatisfaction at the small number of bathing waters identified. These have since been increased.

The sampling procedures laid down in the Directive are not very specific and this had led to wide variations between Member States and also within countries themselves. Some countries take samples at specific times, others base samples on tidal flow (e.g. the UK at high tide), others aim for peak bathing times (Greece). The UK Institute of Environmental Health Officers has called for standardised methodology for sampling and a detailed protocol for analysis. We have our own methodology which allows somewhat less stringent pass criteria for certain beaches.

The Directive does not oblige Member States to provide information relating to the quality of bathing water, although some do so. The UK publishes an annual summary in the *Digest of*

Environmental Protection and Water Statistics which is published by HMSO and is hardly widely available to the average holiday-maker. Denmark publishes a bathing water quality map every year which is shown in schools, libraries and tourist offices, and beaches closed to swimmers are publicised in warnings on the beaches themselves. France displays a similar map in three languages at frontier points.

The Netherlands regularly publishes information on water quality and the Province of South Holland has a hotline to provide information on bathing water standards. Spain publishes no summary covering all its coastal regions, but Greece forbids bathing where adverse results are obtained from sampling. In March 1988, the European Parliament urged the Commission to come forward with a common system of information for bathers on water quality – a common system would have considerable advantages over the present diversity of approach.

This has been, of necessity, a brief look at our obligations to Europe with regard to water, but the various Directives will surface again and again when we look at rivers, estuaries, beaches and tap water and, most of all, at privatisation. For if the European Commission really digs in its heels to force us to bring our water up to a safe and reasonable standard, the cost of so doing will cause the average investor to shudder.

3

Origins of Pollution

If privatisation goes ahead – as it looks as if it will – the new private companies will be taking on, quite literally, a poisoned chalice. Pollution of our waters is now an enormous problem which is getting worse all the time.

The next four chapters will look at rivers, beaches and our tap water. But before doing so it is necessary to take note of the main pollutants and where they come from.

Even our ground water is now polluted. It is contaminated with pesticides and nitrates, and also by unknowns from our virtually unrestricted and uninspected, disgraceful, toxic waste dumps.

The all-party House of Commons Select Committee on the Environment in its report on Toxic Waste (March 1989) was absolutely scathing:

Never in any of our enquiries into environmental problems have we experienced such consistent and universal criticism of existing legislation and of central and local government as we have during the course of this inquiry . . . 56 out of the 79 waste disposal authorities (WDAs) have yet to submit their plans for the disposal of controlled waste in their areas to the Department of the Environment some ten years after legislation required them to do so.

The Department of the Environment has done little or nothing over the years on the issue. Only after the committee began its investigations was a series of measures announced and circulars issued, but, say the committee members cynically, it remains to be seen if anything will come of it and if it is any more than a show of activity while the committee was actually looking into the issue.

It expresses grave concern at what will happen to water once the Water Authorities are privatised and there is no overall body, with real teeth, instead of a national regulatory body which they feel is necessary to oversee toxic wastes.

> The Water Authorities told us that large numbers of landfill sites, mainly older ones, cause local contamination of the groundwater around them. However, they qualified this by saying that they were not aware of *many* [my italics] which actually prejudiced water supplies . . . Once contamination of groundwater has occurred, it is rarely possible to rehabilitate the resource and landfill sites are the most significant threat to groundwater for some Water Authorities. We received evidence that the environmental monitoring at many sites is currently inadequate particularly as regards trace organics.

All kinds of toxic chemicals are carelessly dumped in landfill sites, many of which are hazardous by themselves. By the time they reach the groundwater they have combined into chemical cocktails. We do not even know what is where.

The situation has deteriorated rapidly since 1979. Taking in toxic waste has become big business while the Health and Safety inspectorate side has been allowed to run right down. Following the resignation of the most senior officials and the activities of the Select Committee, we are now told there will be an increase in the number of inspectors – at the end of 1988 they numbered just six to monitor over 5,000 sites.

While the committee dealt with the effects of toxic waste sites on the environment in general, not just water, its findings are obviously applicable to fears of water pollution. It stresses that it recommends the practice now current in the environmentally conscious United States where chemical companies are responsible for their hazardous wastes 'from cradle to grave'. The earlier Royal Commission on Environmental Pollution Report (1985) stated that wastes should be accounted for from the point of production to the point of disposal and subject to adequate evaluation of the disposal route. The Select Committee felt this should be made a strict liability and the waste producers should indeed be responsible for their wastes from 'cradle to grave'. This more than anything, says the committee, 'would ensure that producers consign their wastes to proper persons who, in turn, would be contractually responsible for them'.

Dumping hazardous waste in landfill sites, without their being properly sealed and prepared, is not a popular option elsewhere in Europe, which is why much of it has come to us. Many countries now practice waste minimisation including the substitution of purer or different raw materials, process modifications and recycling within the process. The US Office of Technology Assessment has reviewed waste minimisation in other countries and found that most European governments 'including France, the Federal Republic of Germany, Sweden, Norway, Denmark, the Netherlands and Austria have placed high priority on waste minimisation'. But, guess what, 'their understanding is that the UK has taken little or no action'.

Noting what has happened during the 1980s – the time-bombs of toxic materials sitting in the ground, their possible escape into the atmosphere, into neighbouring land and into ground water – the Select Committee says it was

deeply disturbed by the lack of action by the Department of the Environment in respect of these long acknowledged deficiencies throughout the 1980s. Many of these problems were highlighted in the Gregson Report of 1981, and returned to by the Royal Commission on the Environment in 1985. None of the recommendations in either Report which required legislation has been implemented, although the majority of the recommendations have been accepted by the government. Reviewing progress on much needed legislation since the beginning of the 1980s we find ourselves agreeing with one commentator who said of the Department of the Environment:

'Assessed by concrete results, it can only be judged to have been stone deaf throughout that time to the growing calls, now voiced by every party with an interest in waste management, for regulations to close obvious loopholes in the disposal licensing system, and for primary legislation to extend the framework of control.'

Market forces rule, OK.

So there are unknown quantities of unknown wastes seeping into the ground water. What else is there?

Into ground water and rivers go a variety of substances which will be dealt with in more detail later but they include a wide range of pesticides and herbicides – measurable amounts of Atrazine, Simazine, Mecoprop, 24D, Bromoxynol, Linuron, Chlortoluron, Dieldrin, Trifluralin, 245T, Dicamba, Dichloroprop Dimethoate, MCPA, MCPB and many others were found by Friends of the Earth in water supplies, following an investigation of pesticide pollution in drinking water carried out in 1988 to see how we shaped up to the standards of the EEC Drinking Water Directive.

Some of these, like Dieldrin, are organochlorine nerve-gas derived compounds banned by another EEC Directive in 1979 and still being sold here . . . we are told until stocks run out. Further pressure from the EEC has resulted in the government saying they will be completely phased out by 1992 – just thirteen years later than we were supposed to. 245T is the herbicide which, with 24D, made Agent Orange. This herbicide, with its dioxin contaminant, has possibly had the biggest press of any and is no longer widely used or even made, although we have lagged behind most of the industrialised world in refusing to ban it.

The above substances, together with large quantities of nitrates, now thought to have links with stomach cancers and the 'blue baby syndrome', have reached water supplies and rivers through intensive farming – the intensive farming which has led to food mountains in Europe.

Also into our rivers go a wide variety of metals and chemicals from industry including lead, zinc, cadmium, chlorine, chromium, cyanide, nitrogen, ammonia, etc., etc. They get in there either by direct discharge or via the sewage system. Which brings us to the next pollutant – raw sewage.

Speaking in the famous *Nature* interview on BBC television, on 27 March 1989, Mrs Thatcher 'corrected' Michael Buerk when he pointed out it was hardly a sign of a civilised society that so much sewage ended up in our rivers, on our beaches and dumped out at sea (we are responsible for 90 per cent of the sewage dumped in the North Sea). 'No,' she responded, 'not *raw* sewage . . .' and, as he sought to interject, rolled on in her customary manner . . . 'I think you will find it is *treated sewage*.' It is not, as we shall see, treated sewage.

It is this heady mixture with which the newly privatised companies will be expected to deal. It is also a range of these substances, including lead, nitrates and sewage, on which our lack of action could cause the EEC to throw the spanner into the privatisation works.

4

Rivers of Filth

The control of what goes into our rivers and the condition of them is supposed to be covered by the Control of Pollution Act 1974, known as 'COPA'. It is now generally accepted that this is not a good Act and has loopholes which have allowed rivers to continue to degenerate.

The 1951 Rivers (Prevention of Pollution) Act introduced what is known as a system of 'consents' for the first time. It was supposed to maintain and restore the wholesomeness of rivers, coastal and other inland waterways. It made it an offence to discharge poisonous, noxious or polluting matter into a stream and also an offence to discharge sewage or trade effluent without the consent of the then River Boards. 'Consents', when issued, stipulated the maximum flow to be discharged, the rate at which it could take place and its nature and composition.

As Greenpeace explains in its excellent 1988 report called, appropriately, *Poison in the System*, the Act soon proved difficult to enforce and anyway only controlled discharges to non-tidal streams. It was not until the Clean Rivers and Tidal Waters Act of 1960 was introduced that tidal waters within defined limits were controlled. In addition, the Rivers (Prevention of Pollution) Act 1961 controlled pre-1951 discharges and the Water Resources Act of 1963 controlled discharges of sewage and trade effluent to underground strata by means of wells, boreholes and pipes.

Greenpeace says:

Between 1951 and 1960 many companies took advantage of the almost complete lack of control on discharges to tidal waters and accordingly sited themselves in those areas. Many such companies have remained virtually uncontrolled to this day. Some of those with pre-1951 discharges who applied for consents under the Clean Rivers and Tidal Waters Act 1960 had their application held 'on file' until 1985 They were then given 'deemed consents', which amounts to a virtually free licence to pollute as before.

COPA was supposed to be a logical extension of the previous Acts, extending them to cover discharges to waters not previously controlled.

When the new Water Authorities were formed under the 1974 Water Act they were made responsible for the supply of water, disposal of sewage, land drainage and flood prevention, recreation and amenities including fisheries, and pollution prevention. It then became their duty to grant the 'consents' for discharges and to prosecute offences under the various Rivers Acts.

In 1977, the National Water Council put forward the idea of the River Quality Objective (RQO) where, instead of setting absolute limits, RQOs should be set for rivers and estuaries, and discharges from sewage works and industry would then be set to ensure that the RQOs were met. 'It was thought,' says Greenpeace, 'that this would stop money being wasted on treatment plants which were not needed.' With the adoption of RQOs many sewage works actually received *relaxed* consent conditions.

As Fred Pearce said in *Watershed: The Water Crisis in Britain*, 1982: 'The new consents were not in practice set to meet properly thought out RQOs. They were based on nothing more sophisticated or scientific than the existing standard of the works. A bad works got a loose consent, regardless of the condition of the receiving river.' Britain has consistently argued against the rest of the EEC on the control of discharges into rivers, the EEC favouring fixed standards while we have said the key issue is the effect of the discharge on the receiving water. The European Commission wants overall levels of all chemicals controlled, not just their concentration in specific rivers.

Unfortunately, a compromise was finally reached and members can opt either for absolute control or the UK's approach when implementing EEC Directives on dangerous substances in water.

Note the acronyms COPA and RQO because they will crop up again and again. Our adoption of the system of RQOs, in the late 1970s, presaged the deterioration of rivers in this country for the first time in twenty-five years.

In 1980, the Chairman of the National Water Council said, in the River Quality Report, that 'Control of pollution and river improvement depend both on vigilance and investment'. Greenpeace notes, he went on to say, that 'in the present financial climate there is no prospect of resources available for investment being shifted to this area'.

It must also be noted that the two government departments principally concerned with controlling pollution in rivers are the Department of the Environment (DoE) and the Ministry of Agriculture, Fisheries and Food (MAFF). To date, no Water Authority had been prosecuted by the DoE for illegal sewage discharges although 20 per cent of all discharges in England and Wales were illegal until July 1989, when the Water Authorities were given permission to apply for these discharges to be considered as within legal limits for twelve months.

River Grading

Rivers are graded into four qualities. Grade 1 is high level, suitable for drinking water, fisheries and recreation. Grade 2 is moderate quality, can be used for drinking water after extensive treatment and will still support fish. Grade 3 is poor quality, unsuitable for drinking water abstraction, with fish absent or only occasionally present. Lastly, comes Grade 4, bad quality, grossly polluted, a possible threat to health and to all intents and purposes, dead.

Between 1980 and 1985 there has been a net deterioration of 903 km of rivers. In 1986–7, 4,345 km of rivers were effectively biologically dead and classified as Classes 3–4. That is, 10 per cent of all our rivers. This represents a 3 per cent increase in polluted rivers since 1980. Good quality rivers have declined in length since 1980. In 1986–7, 67 per cent of rivers in England

and Wales were Class 1A and 1B compared to 69 per cent in 1980.

According to Greenpeace, Water Authorities themselves are now a major polluter of our rivers through illegal sewage discharges, despite the review of their consents in 1985. In 1987, more than 20 per cent of sewage works in England and Wales were in breach of their legally binding effluent discharges set by the DoE. 'This,' comments Greenpeace, 'despite the fact that the water authorities are allowed 5% of their samples to fail standards over a period of one year.'

The nation's sewage system has been insufficiently funded for years and particularly so during the last fifteen. By mid-1981 the authorities were investing only £807m in capital projects compared with £1,211m (at today's values) in 1975. Treatment plants just cannot cope and so break down. Some are using equipment sixty or more years old, some are having to serve far larger populations than they were designed for and some are also taking in industrial waste.

Two thousand miles of sewer are officially classified as seriously defective and about 1,300 of the 6,500 sewage works in England and Wales are so inadequate that they break the law. According to a special report in the *Sunday Times* (12 March 1989), Victorian diseases are beginning to return along with Victorian values. Leptospirosis or 'sewerman's disease', contracted from rat's urine, killed fifteen people in 1988. During the month of March, the centre of the city of Manchester virtually ground to a halt when a main sewer burst, and in one area of Plymouth alone houses were flooded with raw sewage five times in a matter of three weeks.

There is also a special link between some industries and Water Authorities so that the industries can use the sewage works, the public not being allowed access to this information. Yet it is recognised that many industrial pollutants cannot be properly treated in existing sewage works. In 1979 and 1985, the Department of the Environment and the Water Authorities actually *relaxed* many of their consents. Environment Minister Nicholas Ridley revealed in Parliament that 1,800 sewage treatment works discharge consents were relaxed between 1984 and 1986, so that

Water Authorities were legally allowed to discharge higher levels of effluent which led, in turn, to industrial users asking for their consents to be relaxed too. In the run-up to privatisation, says Greenpeace, the government is currently considering requests for increasing relaxation of the consents.

If this is agreed then over 2,300 sewage works will be eligible for this special dispensation, so that sewage discharges can be made legal before privatisation.

As has already been noted, a wide range of chemicals pours into our rivers daily. The European Commission on Dangerous Substances has attempted to reduce pollution by certain specific substances and it has drawn up two lists, a Black List (List 1) and a Grey List (List 2). The Black List is composed of the most toxic and persistent substances which include organohalogens, organophosphones and organotin compounds, mercury, cadmium and their compounds. The Grey List includes metals such as zinc, copper nickel, chromium, lead, biocides, cyanide and ammonia. The Directive is designed to get rid of List 1 substances and substantially reduce the pollution from List 2. The adoption of the limitation of amounts of substances and for establishment of Environmental Quality Objectives (EQOs) to List 1 substances entering water is specified in what are known as 'daughter directives'. Daughter directives have already been adopted for mercury, cadmium, the pesticides Lindane, DDT, Dieldrin, Aldrin and Eldrin, pentachlorophenol (PCP) hexachlorobenzene (HCB), hexachlorobutadene (HCBD) and carbon tetrachloride. Within the water covered by the Directive, its adoption must not lead either directly or indirectly to increased pollution.

On 26 February 1989, the *Sunday Times* picked out half a dozen major industrialists for particular mention with regard to pollution of rivers. They were Sir Robert Haslam of British Coal, Sir Kenneth Couzens of Coal Products, Denys Henderson of ICI, Michael Hodgkinson of Express Foods, Kenneth Kemp of British Tissues and Bernard Henderson of the Anglian Water Authority. They were selected on the basis that their companies were among those most frequently prosecuted for pollution offences in the past six years, or most frequently in breach of legally binding limits on the substances which they are allowed to discharge.

This suggests that such polluters are usually penalised in some way. This is not so, however. Between 1980–1 and 1987–8, the number of reported pollution incidents in rivers in England and Wales rose from 12,500 to 23,253. In 1986, only 254 prosecutions were taken out by Water Authorities out of a total of more than 20,000 incidents – an enforcement rate of just 1 per cent. In the Severn Trent Water Authority area alone there were 789 breaches of consents between September 1985 and December 1987, yet only ten prosecutions were brought.

The maximum fine which can be ordered by a Magistrates Court is £2,000 but it is rarely imposed. Fines of around £250 and £500 are far more frequent. Compare this with the United States where criminal penalties are imposed against any person (including responsible corporate officers) who wilfully or negligently violates the Clean Water Act. They are subject to fines of from $2,500 to $25,000 *a day* for each day of violation and/or imprisonment of up to one year. The maximum fines for second offenders are $50,00 *a day* and/or two years in prison!

It is perhaps worth noting here that both benzene and toluene are claimed to be carcinogenic and to cause birth defects and that these substances are found in British rivers, specifically on the Mersey estuary where Norsochem with a 'deemed consent' is situated at West Bank Dock Estate, Widnes. According to the Greenpeace report, the company is currently discharging 4,258 tonnes of Chemical Oxygen Demand (COD) per year, 101.8 tonnes of suspended solids, 29.16 kilograms of cadmium, 14.436 tonnes of iron, 2,916 tonnes of total heavy metals, 1.433 tonnes of cyanide, 508.32 tonnes of ammonia, 16.272 tonnes of benzene, 17.28 tonnes of toluene, 108.0 kilograms of halogenated hydrocarbons (HHCs) and 3.809 tonnes of phenols. The 'deemed consent' for Outfall 1 of Norsochem for Chemical Oxygen Demand (COD) is 6,500 milligrams per litre maximum, yet on 8 July 1987 the company discharged 33,300 mgs per litre. They were not prosecuted for this, they were not even warned by the North West Water Authority.

Meanwhile, joining the flood of chemicals and sewage are the nitrates and yet more pesticides and herbicides coming from farmland.

The government has told us that when water is privatised the situation will improve. It is hard to see why. It also states that the polluter will pay. But the polluters have paid precious little so far while COPA has been in force and much of that act will be lifted straight into the new legislation. West Germany and the Netherlands operate a number of incentive and distributive charging systems along with controls by consents. The distributive charge is designed to help smaller companies and provide a subsidy for pollution control measures. This has led to substantial improvements in the quality of effluent discharged by these countries' industries.

As has already been said, swingeing penalties can be imposed on companies breaking pollution laws in the USA. Also, under the provisions of the Clean Water Act, American citizens can sue waste water dischargers for violating consent limitations. They have to give the discharger a sixty-day notice of intent to sue. When Congress re-enacted the law in 1987 they specifically recognised citizen suits as 'a proven enforcement tool'. Between 1982 and 1984, 214 suits were filed and 800 notices of intent were on record for 1984–7.

There are four possible sanctions that can be enforced against a company – compliance orders which set timetables for achieving compliance; civil actions for appropriate release including a permanent or temporary injunction; civil penalties of up to $10,000 per day per violator; criminal penalties of from $25,000 to $42,500 for a first offence and $50,000 for a second offence and/or imprisonment, as we have already seen, and anyone who knowingly makes a false statement on any document required under the Act may be fined up to $10,000 and/or six months imprisonment.

The law provides for citizen suits, that is, any citizen can commence a civil action against a polluter. They can also sue the Environmental Protection Agency to force them to perform their necessary duties. In this country although there are ways a citizen can sue on an environmental issue, it is very difficult and will probably be extremely expensive as well.

Says Greenpeace: 'It is therefore frustrating that environmental enforcement authorities, such as water authorities, tend to "persuade" polluters rather than take firm action against them.' It is argued that this is more effective than resort to the law but 'the facts to date do not bear this out with regard to industry's high non-compliance with consents and pollution incidents which have occurred due to negligence, carelessness, bad housekeeping, inadequate storage facilities and lack of investment in suitable pollution control technologies'.

In a written answer to the House of Commons Select Committee on the Environment in 1987, the Confederation of British Industry said: 'The UK's present system of water pollution control is working well.' It went on to state that it 'welcomes the steady improvement in the quality of most of the UK's rivers and estuaries'. There would not seem to be the slightest evidence to back up that optimistic statement.

5

Cruising Down the River

The subject of rivers has been split into two chapters in order to look at specific examples in different areas.

The South West Water Authority

In 1986, there were 470 industrial pollution incidents, comprising 21 per cent of the total number of pollution incidents in that area. South West Water prosecuted on only two occasions. In 1986, SWWA tested 229 sewage works and found fifty-five in breach of their 'consents'. Nine people sit on the board of SWWA. In 1987–8, they included the Director of the ICI Group Environmental Laboratory at Brixham, the Chairman and Chief Executive of Blue Circle Cement and the Chairman of Cornwall Business Committee. Conservation interests were represented by the Chairman of the Regional Fisheries Advisory Committee.

The South West sells itself primarily as a tourist area and its publicity shows acres of clean golden beaches into which sparkling clear rivers run. Let us look at a few of them starting in West Cornwall, the 'English Riviera'.

The River Bodilley flows into the bigger River Cober near Wendron, Helston. Until late in 1987 it joined the Cober upstream of an automatic pumping station which syphoned drinking water off to supply the Lizard Peninsula. But increasingly the Bodilley was polluted from slurry and silage draining off from the farms along its banks and when that happened the pumping station's detection system automatically closed the station down and engineers had to go out and clean up the equipment there. In the autumn of 1987, however, it was noted that major works were going on at the pumping station and local people thought this meant that better cleaning equipment was being installed there.

Not so. The Bodilley was diverted into an old mining leet (drain) and then several hundred yards through steel piping until it joined the River Cober downstream of the pumping station. This means that the station no longer closes itself down automatically every time the Bodilley becomes severely polluted – but the pollution has not gone away. Fish die, trout farms drawing supplies from the Cober find their filters are always in trouble, and eventually the polluted water makes its way down to one of the National Trust's great beauty spots, the Loe Pool. In September 1988, there was a major pollution incident in the Bodilley which killed off most of the river's fish. Only after media publicity was any action taken and eventually a farmer was warned for allowing slurry to contaminate the water.

On the Saturday of the August Bank Holiday weekend 1987, the Coombe River,which flows into Newlyn Harbour near Penzance, was choked with dead fish and eels, everything from the smallest to the largest. At first South West Water disclaimed any knowledge of the incident but finally told the writer that pollution was probably coming from a small industrial estate upstream. We followed the river right back to where it emerged from SWWA's Drift Reservoir and the fish had died all the way along its length. Eventually, SWWA admitted there had been a mistake and that operatives had released a substance into the river when cleaning out tanks. We were never told what. A year later came the notorious Lowermoor Treatment Works incident in North Cornwall when aluminium sulphate was wrongly tipped into the purified water supply.

Now, however, the pretty Coombe River is thoroughly contaminated – with pesticides from the flower growers and from offal from the abattoir on the industrial estate. It now sports notices saying that the water is contaminated and that it is not safe to fish in it.

So to glorious Devon. The Tamar and Torridge Rivers and their tributaries are now so contaminated with farm waste that it will take years for them to run clean again, if they ever will. The South West has the worst farm pollution figures in the country with 230 miles of Grade 1 rivers (14 per cent) being downgraded in just one year. In North Devon, Hillsdown Holdings, one of the country's largest farming and food groups, has a slaughterhouse at Torrington. Last year they were convicted on three separate charges of pouring abattoir waste and sludge into a tributary of the Torridge.

Farm waste, especially slurry, is now one of the fastest growing pollution problems in the country, nowhere more so than Somerset. On 5 March 1989, the *Sunday Times* carried the story of the pollution of the moat at Stogursey Castle in the Quantocks where all the Chinese grass carp died. The pollution came from the Stogursey brook into which poured slurry from Cricket Malherbie Farms. In 1987, its chairman, Metford Jeanes, was fined £4,000 for three separate offences. He had already been fined before in 1986, 1984 and 1983.

The trouble has been caused by his huge herd of cows, now some 360-strong, occupying two different farm sites, along with 3,000 pigs which are on a third of the area. These animals, says the report, generate so much waste which is so powerful that it would take the human sewage of Cardiff and Swansea combined to equal his animals' potential damage to the environment.

He feeds the animals, as do many farmers nowadays, on silage and that too drains from containers into rivers. Silage is 200 times more damaging than sewage beause the microorganisms that feed on it rapidly remove oxygen from the water thus killing the fish. But Jeanes' main problem appears to be the slurry which is dealt with in today's way by putting it into slurry lagoons. The lagoons hold gallons of animal faeces and urine. The *Sunday Times* notes that had Mr Jeanes been a motorist and clocked up so many offences he would probably have lost his licence. As it is, he has nothing to worry about and told the paper: 'Look, it's cheap money. When you have a problem that could take £200,000 to solve, £2,000 is cheap money.'

Overall, the average prosecution rate for farmers has been 5 per cent of all known pollution cases and in the South West fines have been as low as £25 or farmers have merely been slapped on the wrist and conditionally discharged.

Before leaving the South West it is as well to take a brief look at the River Severn (which actually comes under the Severn Trent Water Authority) which will be discussed in more detail in the chapter on estuaries and beaches. Rivers draining into the estuary currently carry with them measurable levels of mercury, cadmium, lead and zinc.

The Yorkshire Water Authority

In 1980, there were 1,071 pollution incidents in this area and thirty-nine prosecutions – 3.6 per cent. Pollution dropped slightly until 1984 and then began to rise rapidly. By 1987, there were 2,325 incidents and then began to rise rapidly. There were also 763 breaches of consents but only eleven prosecutions. Among the twelve people sitting on the board of YWA in 1987–8 were Gordon Jones, chairman of the YWA and of the Water Authorities Association, a former managing director of various steel and engineering companies and manager of Esso Petroleum's Industrial Sales, a former director of British Petroleum, a former managing director of BP Chemicals in Belgium and, once again, conservation interests were represented by a member of the Regional Fisheries Advisory Committee.

Continuing its investigations into the state of rivers, the *Sunday Times*, on 12 March 1988, looked at the problems facing publican Peter Hardy who runs a pub next to the Bradford Beck. The contents of some 200,000 lavatories overflow from the sewers into his stream and from thence into local rivers. The stream regularly carries condoms, tampon holders and so many human faeces that locals call them 'the Barnsley trout'. When the reporter visited Mr Hardy a dead Alsatian was lying in the water – it had been there for two weeks. Questioned about the Bradford Beck, a spokesman for YWA told the *Sunday Times* that the problem is caused by storm sewers which should work only during storms but which are open constantly owing to the amount of sewage discharging every day. It will be eight to ten years before they can be replaced. 'There has been a starvation of funds for sewerage and sewage treatment. Now we are paying the price.'

Still in Yorkshire, the River Don runs brown and strong smelling. It starts off clean enough in a Pennine reservoir but by the time it reaches Oughtibridge, near Sheffield, it is virtually starved of oxygen. Among those pumping waste into the Don are British Tissues and as the river flows past the factory it drops from Grade 2 to Grade 4. According to YWA, fourteen out of twenty-seven samples taken at Oughtibridge in 1988 were illegal but the firm has not been prosecuted since 1983. All the dyes used in lavatory papers stain the river and the bed is covered in rotting paper.

Flowing into the Don is the Rother which is, according to Greenpeace, the longest stretch of grossly polluted river in the country – dead for two-thirds of its thirty-one miles. It is polluted by old iron ore workings as it rises from the ground. It then flows past the Avenue coking plant at Wingerworth in Derbyshire, where it changes from an ochre colour to a darker shade owing to the rich tarry waste from the plant. Two years ago the company arranged to have some of its worst effluent pumped into the Old Whittington sewage works but ammonia still leaks into the Rother. Coal Products breached its consents twelve times out of the seventeen times it was tested.

Downstream the same sewage works mentioned above discharges dark brown effluent containing high levels of ammonia into the river. By this time the river is classified as Grade 4 – quite dead. The discharges from the overloaded sewage works contained an average of 20 milligrams per litre of ammonia. Five mg/l are enough to kill off all animal life. Into the Rother flows the Doe Lea stream into which Coalite discharges hundreds of gallons of process waste.

Next stop is Staveley Chemicals owned by Rio Tinto Zinc. It makes caustic soda and benzene and it pumps a mixture of ammonia, chlorine and heavy metals into the water. In 1987, Stavely Chemicals spent £1.3m on a plant to reduce mercury in its effluent but this has not fully solved the problem. Just outside Sheffield the Rother flows through the Rother Valley Country Park. Finally, on to Orgreave where British Steel made profits of £419m in 1988 and spent just £85,000 on a new treatment plant. In 1974, YWA said the Rother would be a Grade 2 river by 1979. In 1979, the date was put back to 1987. Now it stands at 2001.

North West Water

In 1980, there were 1,332 pollution incidents of which nineteen were prosecuted – 1.4 per cent. In 1986, there were 2,480 incidents of which twenty-two were prosecuted – just *0.9 per cent*. In 1987–8, there were ten members on NWWA's Board including a former Senior Commercial Advisor to Esso Europe, a President of the British Paper and Board Industry Federation, a Counsellor on the Department of Trade and Industry's Enterprise Initiative and, yes, you've guessed it, a member of the Fisheries Advisory Committee.

According to Greenpeace, evidence from NWWA shows that when COPA was implemented, rather than effect an improvement in water quality, consents for industrial discharges were actually relaxed in order to allow companies to emit legal amounts of effluent and make them immune from prosecution. In spite of this there is evidence that companies actually breach these much relaxed consents.

The River Goyt flows into the Mersey which, in turn, flows into the Irish Sea. It rises in the Peak District, flows into two reservoirs and continues on its way, a source of pleasure for trout fishers. A few hundred yards further on it becomes poisoned, the water turns a milky white from which comes an evil smell. Fish vanish. Within yards the river has changed from Grade 1 to Grade 4. Edward Hall and Brothers, manufacturers of bleached cotton, use most of the river (some 2.5m gallons a day) in their processing plant. The water is then returned full of dyes and bleach. The NWWA say that the discharge of 'trade effluent' is quite legal. In fact the authority has been very kind to Halls, first allowing it a consent to discharge 40 milligrams per litre of suspended solids into the river and then upping that to 60. It now stands at 50 mg/l. In spite of this the factory still breaks the law but has not been prosecuted. The Goyt is then joined by a polluted tributary, the Black Brook.

The Black Brook also starts clean in the Peak District but becomes polluted with effluent from Coates Viyella. The factory used to send its effluent to the local sewage works which can no longer cope with the amount and so the effluent is put through an outdated plant and back into the Black Brook. According to NWAA, eleven out of fifteen samples of waste taken from the factory last year were illegal – discharges include permanganate – but the factory was not prosecuted. One reason apparently is that NWWA's own plant at Chapel-en-le-Frith pollutes the Black Brook so heavily that there is little point in getting the factories to clean up their act. A few hundred yards further on Ferodo, which makes brake linings, releases up to forty times as much formaldehyde and twice as much phenol as it should into the Brook without fear of prosecution. When the Black Brook and Goyt join together suds on the surface can reach 6 feet in height and are often brightly coloured as foaming discharge from Whaley Bridge sewage works joins everything else. The sewage works is allowed to dump 45 mg/l of suspended solids into the river. In March 1988, samples taken showed a concentration of 860 mg/l.

A cleaner river then flows into the Goyt, diluting it somewhat but soon it passes Strines Textiles of Marple which discharge bleaches and dyes. This company broke the law five times in 1988 but, as usual, was not prosecuted. Eventually, as the *Sunday Times* pointed out, the Goyt flows into the Mersey carrying with it the pollutants from Hall, Coats Viyella, Ferodo, the sewage works, Strines *et al.*, to add to those flowing in from a dozen other rivers and 200 industrial discharge pipes. The whole lot flows past Norsochem which has already been mentioned as discharging a cocktail of metals and chemicals into the Mersey, including the dangerous benzene and toluene.

The chief scientist of NWAA said: 'We know it's a bloody disgrace but there's no point in wasting valuable time and resources sampling something bloody awful.'

It would be possible to go through all ten areas served by the Water Authorities in this way but I will finish with just one.

Thames Water Authority

In 1980, there were 1930 pollution incidents in the TWA of which six were prosecuted – 0.3 per cent. In 1986, there were 2,890 incidents of which twelve were prosecuted – 0.4 per cent. What price improvement!

What better place to start with Thames Water than Finchley, constituency of our own, newly greened, Prime Minister. Dollis Brook lies in the very heart of Finchley. Under the headline *The Blot on Thatcher's Landscape*, the 5 March 1989 edition of *The Observer* showed a pool, surrounded by pleasant trees, on the banks of which was stuck a large notice saying, 'Danger – Polluted Water. Keep Clear'. It was polluted by Finchley's sewage system which broke down in February 1989 and now the council has had to put up the signs telling people to keep away.

The paper quotes Mr Brian Watkins, chairman of the local residents' association as saying:

> You'll learn more about what she *really* feels about the environment from this than from any number of words she comes out with at today's much-publicised Ozone Conference ... Mrs Thatcher has probably never even seen it but, you know, it used to be one of the most beautiful spots in the area. There used to be herons and Canada geese here.
>
> I saw a man come down to the Brook and he looked at it and burst into tears. He told me he had played beside it as a child and he had been visiting it ever since. He just couldn't believe what had happened.

In February 1989, the River Wey, near Godalming, was found

to be polluted with two highly dangerous toxic chemicals – Lindane and Tributyltin Oxide (TBTO), both used as wood preservatives. It was the second incident within days. The first concerned 3,000 gallons of oil which came from a nearby industrial estate. The Wey flows into the Thames. Andrew Lees of Friends of the Earth, quoted in *The Observer* (19 February 1989), said: 'This incident will leave a toxic legacy which will harm wildlife for many years to come. These incidents have happened before.' The technical manager of a company which banned both these chemicals in 1986 after fears over their safety said: 'There is no doubt that this is a major pollution incident. The chemicals will seep into the soil and fish will die. Birds that eat the fish will also be affected.' A spokesman for Thames Water said they had acted to close Thames Water intakes downstream from the incident but there was a possibility that one intake – which supplies domestic water – might have been contaminated.

Thames Water does not make much information available to the public and gives no overall information at all on compliance for industrial discharges to rivers and sewers.

Like all rivers the Thames suffers from a variety of pollutants. Raw sewage floods into it upstream (a group of private citizens successfully prosecuted Thames Water in January 1989) and where it passes the Aldermaston nuclear plant, radioactive water. In 1982, old buildings at Aldermaston were reopened to produce plutonium for Chevaline warheads – they had previously been closed down in 1978 due to contamination. Some 1 million gallons of plutonium-contaminated water a year is pumped into the Thames near Pangbourne. Yorkshire Television holds a document which states that the waste treatment plant does not conform with current safety standards.

Two warning signs are placed on the river bank at the outflow warning people not to moor, anchor or bathe between these signs. Questioned about the contaminated outflow on television, on 3 March 1985, Defence Minister Lord Trefgarne said: 'I'm told that if you drink a pint of the effluent from Aldermaston that goes into the river – in radioactivity terms at least – it is no more dangerous than a pint of mineral water purchased over the counter of your local supermarket.' Unfortunately, nobody asked him to prove his confidence by swigging a pint of it.

Pollution of the Thames is not, as already mentioned, a modern phenomenon. The Romans used it as a sewer and it was concern over the state of some of its tributaries which caused Richard II to attempt to force improvements. An Act passed in 1847 to stem the tide of overflowing private cesspools and for such drainage to be connected with street sewers resulted only in an ever greater amount of domestic refuse being dumped in the Thames. The great cholera outbreaks of the nineteenth century were a direct result of drinking water being extracted from the river's polluted waters.

Since 1889 special barges have carried away sludge and sewage down the Thames and dumped it offshore in the North Sea. This did result, for a short while, in the river becoming cleaner but by the 1930s it was rapidly deteriorating again. However, sewage still flows into the Thames from several outfalls and, because of the tidal flow, travels only relatively slowly to the sea. Measurements taken at Teddington Weir (*The Thames Estuary – A Current Status Research Report*, Greenpeace, 1986) show that effluent discharged from the northern outfall takes twenty days to travel 32 kilometres seawards. The RQO was set as 'a minimum dissolved oxygen level of 10% of air saturation at all times and places in the estuary'. The report says:

> It was generally shown to being equivalent to an average level of oxygen over any three-month period of at least 30% air saturation, which was considered as sufficient for the passage of migrating fish by the Thames Migratory Fish Committee. This may be true but for the resident population of fish and the invertebrates, of course, neither the average value nor the 95% minimum has any meaning.

The report goes on to accuse TWA of 'environmental brinkmanship' which would be dangerous enough with a quality standard with built-in safety factors, but with such a low objective it is even more worrying to find that even this limit has been breached on a number of occasions. The report concludes:

Finally, there is also evidence from sources within Thames Water that on more than one occasion aeration plants at the major sewage works at Beckton, Crossness and Mogden, have been temporarily shut down in order to save money. Such irresponsible action does nothing to help increase the oxygen content of the water since untreated sewage has an even greater oxygen depleting influence than treated effluent.

The Thames is one of the worst offenders for heavy metal dissemination through contaminated sludge dumping in its estuary. TWA's sewage works regularly handle industrial mercury and cadmium wastes well above what are supposed to be EEC limits. Grey List metals found in the Thames include copper, zinc, lead and mercury. High levels of mercury have been found in fish in the estuary. Also by the time the Thames has reached its estuary it also contains Lindane, Aldrin, Dieldrin, Endrin, DDT, and PCBs – polychlorinated biphenyls. These too have been found in fish.

In a note on some of the Thames tributaries the previously quoted report says: 'The urban rivers, the tributaries which drain into the lower reaches of the Thames have been labelled as "disasters" even by scientists employed by the Thames Water Authority. This is principally because of intensive flood alleviation schemes, urban run-off and general neglect. The Rivers Ravensbourne, Beverley, Wandle and Brent catchments are particularly bad.'

The Ravensbourne (called 'the Forgotten River' rises in Bromley and enters the Thames at Deptford. Only 30 per cent remains in its natural state, the rest is buried in tunnels or channels which virtually deprive it of any natural life. The River Quality Objective (RQO) is at fault concerning these neglected rivers, since the objective (as with the Thames itself and other waterways) is chosen according to the quality achievable under *present* conditions. As funds are not being allocated for actually upgrading, a Grade 3 river will stay Grade 3 and as long as the quality objective is not met, no effort is made to reduce pollution as long as it does not degrade itself to Grade 4.

Perhaps we should leave the Thames with a note about the

famous salmon. Plentiful supplies of these fish do not seem to have been reliably reported since the seventeenth century. Now we are told, often by government ministers, that the Thames has been so cleaned up that salmon are once more to be found there. The reality is slightly different. Attempts were made to restock in 1862–4 and again in 1900 but both failed owing to the state of the Thames. Experimental stocking has been carried out since 1974 on the Pang and the Eye in the headwaters of the Thames and experience does not seem to bear out the belief, now widely held, that the Thames is leaping with salmon. A Dr Alwyne Wheeler, commenting on the position with regard to restocking in 1974, said that only two were found from this attempt – one was dead and another was later seen leaping at Shepperton Weir but eventually found dead in the same pool in September 1978.

In May 1979, another attempt was made with the introduction of 50,000 yearlings from Scotland. Between 1980 and 1982 there were twenty-one sightings of salmon – only three were positively identified as adults as opposed to young ones migrating to the sea from subsequent introductions later than 1979. Young salmon smolts have continued to be introduced into the Thames. In 1985, eleven salmon were caught in the Thames – similar to the number caught back in 1812 when the river was supposed to have been at its most polluted.

It would be possible to go on and on and into more detail about other Water Authority areas. For example, Severn Trent Water holds the record for the highest number of pollution incidents in 1988 – 900. Its sewage treatment works actually made a profit of £157m for the authority from charges to companies using public drains, making it the most profitable service run by any Water Authority. Anglian Water's sewage works have the worst record in England and Wales. In 1987, one in three of its sewage works operated illegally. Northumbrian Water is the least likely to take polluters to court to protect its rivers. There were 700 pollution incidents in 1986 and it prosecuted just once – a Middlesbrough farmer who was fined £50. In 1987, there were 671 pollution incidents, a third of them caused by Northumbrian Water itself. And back again to Thames Water, known as the 'privatisation flagship' – nearly one in five of its sewage works broke the law in 1987, being responsible for 423 pollution incidents. The River Lee, which is a main source of potable water for North London, can, during summer months and in dry weather conditions, be composed of up to 60 per cent of sewage effluent.

As the Greenpeace report concludes: 'Basically, the wrong thinking here by the Water Authorities is that the only incentive to maintain the quality of rivers and ground water is the need to extract a potable supply. Not all rivers, however, are water supply rivers. The incentive should be on environmental protection.'

Can we really believe that privatisation will improve our rivers or that shareholders will be prepared to see the private companies spend the vast amount of money now needed to clean them up?

6

On the Beach

Oh, I do like to be beside the seaside,
Oh, I do like to be beside the sea . . .

goes the old music-hall song. It conjures up a picture of golden Edwardian summers, frilly bathing dresses and mashers in straw boaters. The bleak reality today is that on most of our beaches you have to pick your way through plastic detritus, litter and tar at best, and at worst all that plus crude sewage too, along with things we cannot see but are in the water anyway.

For instance, there are a number of well-known holiday resorts that face on to the Irish Sea – Blackpool, Fleetwood and Morecambe to name but three of them. Nine million people visit what has become known as the 'sea of filth' for their holidays.

Greenpeace provide some statistics. It contains more man-made radioactivity than any other sea in the world and is the dumping ground for 80 tonnes a year of natural uranium. The biggest industrial dump in the North Atlantic is a few miles from the city of Cork. In the Severn estuary, zinc levels thirty times higher than in the Atlantic have been measured, 125 times the amount of lead and 250 times the amount of cadmium. These flow into the sea from the Severn, courtesy of the Severn Trent Water Authority. From Britain's dirtiest estuary, the Mersey, come the heavy metals and chemicals already referred to, courtesy of the North West Water Authority whose sewage treatment works receive more industrial effluent than any other authority in the UK – nearly 250 million litres a day.

The equivalent of a truckload of industrial waste is dumped into the Irish Sea every minute all the year round. A million tonnes of industrial waste alone go into the dumping site near Cork each year – 3.5 tonnes per minute. Four million tons of sewage sludge a year are dumped in the Irish Sea. Off Garroch Head in Scotland, a layer of 15 centimetres deep covers an area of 10 kilometres of the seabed. 'Bacteria in sludge,' says Greenpeace, 'can remain dormant for over a year and then pass genetic information on to marine bacteria. It's possible for new bacteria strains to evolve. No one can guess at the effects on shellfish and on the humans who eat them – something to think about while you enjoy your fish and chips after a dip in the sea.'

Addressing that strange body, the Conservative Central Committee at Scarborough, on 18 March 1989, the Prime Minister extolled the virtues of water privatisation emphasising the improvement it would have on the environment. She chose an unfortunate place to make such a statement for even now the Yorkshire Water Authority is working on a pipe to take yet more sewage out into the sea only half a mile off the coast from where the conference was taking place.

When the European Commission had got over our little joke about how many designated bathing beaches we had (our original figure, less than Luxembourg as already noted, was twenty-seven), we then had to come up with a more realistic figure and this now stands at 380. Department of the Environment figures say that in 1988 67 per cent of the waters tested met European quality standards and 'improvement schemes are in hand or planned, with the aim of bringing the remaining waters up to these standards by 1995'.

The statement continues: 'The results of the survey carried out during the 1988 bathing season show that 67% of our bathing waters in England, Wales and Northern Ireland met the mandatory coliform bacteria standards of the EEC Bathing Water Directive. This represents a significant improvement over 1987 when, measured on the same basis, only 55% of our waters met these standards.' Standards, continues the DoE, have been tightened up, monitoring improved and 'measured on the new basis, 254 out of the 380 bathing waters in England, Northern Ireland and Wales met the Directive's mandatory standards during the 1988 bathing season. This compares with 206 out of 370 waters (55%) in 1987 and 184 out of 358 waters (51%) in 1986.' Which is an improvement.

While this picture is supported by the figures also given by the Marine Conservation Society, the latter's statistics show that there is rather more to it. The society rightly prides itself on the work it has done to press for cleaner beaches and notes that it was its provision of information to the EEC which compelled the government to include a further 350 beaches in their list of bathing waters. The society monitored just over 500 sites in 1988 and found that 193, or 38 per cent of them, failed to meet the minimum EC standard for clean bathing beaches. In some areas, well over half of the beaches monitored failed the test. 'On many beaches, even those complying with the European Commission standards, sewage is released with no treatment at all, the waste, including nuisance solids, is released directly into the sea.'

The sewage from 6.394 million people in the UK, approximately 13 per cent of the entire resident population, is discharged through sea outfalls and it has been established that this figure doubles during the summer. There are over 400 outfalls discharging sewage into coastal waters which receive varying degrees of treatment. Over 70 per cent of sewage receives either no treatment at all or only preliminary treatment such as maceration (breaking up the solids to make them smaller). In 1973, a DoE review showed that 61 per cent of sewage outfalls discharge at, or above, low water mark. Less than 8 per cent of outfalls could be considered to be long sea outfalls and, says the Marine Conservation Society, little has changed since then. The Water Research Centre identified 191 beaches that are in the vicinity of an outfall which serves more than 2,000 people.

Back in the mid-1960s, the author researched a programme for the now defunct Westward Television and it was filmed at the end of an outfall pipe which flowed into the sea just off the holiday beach of Marazion, in Cornwall. Raw sewage floated in the water and a number of unpleasant bacteria were found to be present in it. Twenty-five years later the pipe is still there, serving a vastly increased population. The beach is no longer just covered with human excrement – added to it now are condoms, lavatory paper, used sanitary towels and the ubiquitous 'disposable' nappy. South West Water is planning to improve matters with a super outfall pipe which will collect sewage from a wider area and then pump all of it out to sea!

Among the many famous beaches considered to be below minimum European Commission standards are the following, together with their relevant Water Authorities:

Wessex Water (North Coast):   Weston-super-Mare, Burnham-on-Sea, Minehead;
South West Water: Ilfracombe, Bude, St Ives (Porthgwidden), Marazion and Mount's Bay, Porthallow, Plymouth Hoe, Salcombe South, Paignton, Teignmouth, Budleigh Salterton and Lyme Regis;
Southern Water: Christchurch Bay, Ventnor, Whitecliffe Bay, Ryde, Cowes, Southsea, Selsey, Littlehampton, Worthing, Hove, Brighton, Newhaven, Hastings, Dymchurch, Hythe, Folkestone, Sandwich Bay, Ramsgate and Herne Bay;
Anglian Water: Leigh-on-Sea, Southend (both Thorpe Bay and Westcliffe), Great Yarmouth, Hunstanton and Cleethorpes;
North West Water: St Bees, Morecambe, Fleetwood, Blackpool, St Annes and Southport;
Wales: Prestatyn (Barkby), Rhyl, Abergele, Colwyn Bay (Calyley Prom), Llandudno (West Shore), Morfa Conwy, Llanfairfechan, Pwllheli, Criccieth West, Aberdovey, Aberystwyth, Aberporth, Tenby (North), Saundersfoot, Llanelli, Swansea Bay, Aberafon (East) and Margam Sands;
Northern Ireland: Ballycastle, Ballyhome and Newcastle;
Scotland. Forth Area: Milsey Bay Broadsands, Shell Bay;
Tay Area: St Andrews, Arbroath;
Highlands: Nairn and Invergordon.

There are many, many more but this is just to give an idea. In passing, Scottish beaches seem to be less polluted than those elsewhere.

And what else can we find on the beach? The House of Commons Select Committee on the Environment, when looking into toxic and hazardous wastes, refers to Seaham Harbour in County Durham in these terms.

> Some of us visited Seaham Harbour in County Durham and saw the effects of colliery spoil and slurry disposal on the beach. Colliery spoil and washery slurry are not controlled wastes under COPA 1974, but are deposited under licence from MAFF and the Northumbrian Water Authority. The problem of their disposal therefore falls outside the scope of our inquiry but it raises important questions of pollution control.
>
> We were appalled by the impact of dumping on the Durham beaches; and we understand that, although attempts have been made over a number of years to resolve the situation, there is no immediate prospect of an end to it. We were told that the economics of production on the Durham and Northumberland coalfields were such that an end to dumping of spoil on the beaches now would render the pits unprofitable. It seems to us that the situation has been allowed to develop because the agencies which originally permitted this method of disposal had no particular commitment to environmental protection. The unfortunate situation which has resulted is an added demonstration of the need for a strong and independent Environmental Protection Commission. We recommend that responsibility for the regulation of dumping of colliery waste at sea or on the foreshore should be transferred from MAFF and the Northumberland Water Authority to Her Majesty's Inspectorate of Pollution.

The resorts bordering on the Severn estuary receive a wide range of pollutants. On the north side are the old industrialised areas of South Wales with their history of mining and metal processing. On the southern shore are the smelting and chemical processing plants of Avonmouth and Severnside along with three nuclear power stations – Hinkley, Berkeley and Oldbury. Sewage, as we have seen, is a problem in the area – sewage from Cardiff, Newport, Swansea and Bristol makes its way to the river after varying degrees of treatment.

As mentioned previously, the rivers draining into the Severn bring down a further flood of pollutants from pesticides to toxic metals. Cadmium causes the greatest concern as it is found in the most concentrated levels but the rising levels of zinc, mercury and lead are also worrying. Amounts of all these have been found in fish and shellfish taken from the river estuary.

Some of the metal contamination in the river comes from old mine workings in North Devon and parts of Somerset and the old waste tips of the Swansea valley, and the land contaminated by past industrial processes also adds to the amounts. But added to these are pollutants from current and recent waste tips together with the industrial charges we know go into rivers and public sewers now that it is becoming positively *profitable* for Water Authorities to undertake this service for industrial users.

Exactly what the effect on human health of all this is is difficult to quantify, but the next time you decide to plunge into the briny along the Severn estuary take a thought of what is going into it.

Lastly, to the most hidden beach hazard of all – radiation. Several years ago this writer visited the beautiful beach below the Sellafield nuclear plant with scientists from Lancaster University who took geiger counters – the readings went off the scale. This was before the famous incident on 11 November 1983 when something went badly wrong and radioactive water was flushed out into the Irish Sea. The general public was not informed for four days and only then because Greenpeace was in the area. On the 7 December, the government had to issue a warning to the public not to use the beaches along a twenty-five-mile stretch of coastline. Up to 1,000 times the normal background radiation was found on some sections of the beach. Radioactive particles were still being found on parts of the beach in March of the following year.

Perhaps this last seems an unlikely hazard but it is worth remembering the story of Dr Barry Matthews who had received international recognition for his work in the Arctic. He was with the Agriculture Research Council's soil survey team in 1977, working in West Cumbria. It was already known that the beaches in the area were contaminated with radioactive material washed back on to them on the tide that was supposed to have washed it out into the Irish Sea. He became more and more worried and, by 1979, was particularly alarmed at a 'hot spot' he found near the Drigg Brook. He told British Nuclear Fuels at Sellafield of his concern but they assured him there was no cause for alarm and radioactivity was well within permissible limits.

He took sand samples and became even more concerned. Finally, finding some people having a picnic near to the place he had found particularly contaminated, he warned them that he did not think it was a suitable place for children to play because of radioactive contamination. The family took the hint and went further, taking the matter up with their MP who then got in touch with British Nuclear Fuels. Dr Matthews stuck to his guns, backed up by independent research from Manchester University which had shown radiation levels on the public beach to be up to 100 times the background level. But in April 1981 Dr Matthews was hauled up before an industrial tribunal and charged with a number of offences including using his official position in an unauthorised way to give an unwarranted warning to the family on the beach. On 18 June 1981, he was sacked. Eventually, after various tribunals and legal action it was found that he had been wrongfully dismissed and he was awarded damages. But he never got his job back.

Anxiety does not end there. Cumbrian rivers come under the North West Water Authority and this includes the River Esk which flows into the sea at Ravenglass. Radioactive pollution has been found in the Ravenglass estuary for many years now and in February 1989 Friends of the Earth revealed new high levels of caesium 137 up to 4,400 becquerels per kilogram compared with the National Radiological Protection Board's limit of 900. Americium 241, a particularly dangerous isotope associated with plutonium, was found at levels of up to 2,900 bqs per kilogram compared with the National Radiological Protection Board's limit of 1,000. The NRPB says that when levels reach *a quarter* of their limits, the doses received by people most likely to be affected should be investigated. The amounts in the FoE samples were ten to twenty times more than that. Gamma radiation measurements further up the river, some three miles upstream, were between two and five times the usual background level.

FoE were concerned that anyone spending twenty hours a week on the river bank would exceed the NRPB's recommended safety limit with the additional risk of inhaling the tiny radioactive particles which can be blown into the air from dried mud and sand in the summer. FoE felt there should be an immediate investigation of the state of the Ravenglass estuary as 'information like this could provide the key to the cause of the increased incidents of childhood leukeamia locally'. It was felt that this was urgent to see if local people were being exposed to dangerous levels.

The response from the authorities was summed up by MAFF. A spokeswoman told *The Guardian*, which carried the report on 6 February 1989, that: 'We would welcome any data that people might present that would help ensure public safety. But so far we've not seen any evidence to suggest that our monitoring is in the wrong places or that any particular product that may be contaminated has been missed . . . levels obviously vary but continuous individual assessments confirm the absence of any cause for concern.'

Beach pollution, unfortunately, becomes the responsibility of a number of organisations – first the Water Authorities, then local authorities, MAFF and, in special circumstances, industries such as British Nuclear Fuels. The only logical way out of a situation where it is all too easy for one to pass the buck to the other is, as the House of Commons Select Committee suggested, to put the beaches under the overall control of the Pollution Inspectorate.

7

Poison on Tap

The following quote is from a letter which appeared in the April 1989 edition of *Good Housekeeping* following a previous article on tap water.

> You should try the tap water in Newcastle-on-Tyne! Go away on holiday and a brown residue forms around the water level in the loo. If we're lucky, we get fizzy water from our taps – no need for Perrier. The washing machine intake is brown, and when the bathwater is let out a black grit remains in the bottom of the bath – not, I can assure you, from me. To test the situation, we installed a fibre filter, which was covered in black sludge within two weeks . . .

The state of our tap water is now such that there hardly seems to be a day, let alone a week, when the subject does not arise somewhere in the media and increasingly in the women's magazines like *She*, *Good Housekeeping* and *Woman* and glossies such as *Country Living*.

Anthony Tucker, writing in *The Guardian* (21 March 1989) on microbes and suchlike in our water, puts it well:

> A century of inadequate maintenance plus the absolute neglect through Government parsimony a decade ago has left a maintenance deficit of around £25 billion. With old water mains throbbing with niches awaiting microbial occupants, old towns criss-

crossed with long forgotten and disused underground drains and piping, the rivers increasingly fouled by legal and illegal discharges of human and animal sewage, the truly amazing thing is that parasitic diseases are not more widespread.

So many different things now go into our tap water that it is necessary to split this chapter into sections.

Microbes, Bacteria and Other Nasties

'Polluted Water Supplies Blamed for Sickness', ran the headlines in the newspapers towards the end of February 1989. Over a hundred people had been affected with sickness and diarrhoea in Oxfordshire and Wiltshire. The cause turned out to be an animal parasite called cryptosporidia which had infected the Farmoor water works in Oxford which comes under the aegis of Thames Water. The alert was first raised by the Community Medicine team at Swindon because, during a screening programme being carried out there, it had been noticed that the number of cases of cryptosporidiosis was rising rapidly.

While for most people this disease is merely unpleasant but not serious, there are vulnerable groups including the very young, and it can also be a serious, and sometimes fatal, illness in those people whose immuno-suppression systems are poor such as AIDS sufferers and those on immuno-suppressive drugs. It appeared that the organism had built up in the water plant's filters. As to where it came from – the plant takes its water from the Thames where it could well be present and it is known to be present in animal slurries and possibly in human sewage sludge.

To return to Anthony Tucker, he points out that there has never been routine monitoring for these pathogenic protozoa in drinking water, and, in general, Water Authorities have neither the expertise nor the facilities and time to carry out the painstaking investigations needed to ensure a continuous high level of control.

About 20,000 people were at risk in this outbreak. There had also been an earlier one in Ayrshire, in 1988, which was attributed after lengthy investigations to the contamination of treated drinking water by effluent from a forgotten clay pipe which drained land treated with cattle slurry. A larger outbreak in Sheffield, in 1986, was never satisfactorily explained. Tucker also refers to a mysterious waterborne infection which hit 3,000 people in Leeds, in 1980, and was susbequently interpreted as having been caused by a parasite. It might have been caused by the Giardia organism. This organism affixes itself in large numbers to the lining of the gut and can be hard to get rid of and, in some cases, even life threatening.

The number of cases of giardiosis among those who have not travelled abroad is on the increase, at the same time as illegal discharges of farm slurry has reached a new high. Some experts now think that modern farm slurry discharges could be a key factor in rising infection rates.

The above outbreaks at least have been properly noted and efforts made to trace their causes but there are increasing reports of waves of sickness and diaorrhea, particularly affecting young children, in other parts of the country. Mothers in the Newlyn–Penzance area of West Cornwall, for example, are concerned at their frequency and the lack of explanation for them and some have taken to using water filters as a result.

In his report, Anthony Tucker says that after the Ayrshire incident, the Scottish Home and Health Department put up money to extend studies of parasitic protozoa already being carried out in universities and laboratories in Scotland, and noting that Strathclyde's investigations over the past couple of years have confirmed the prevalence of viable parasite cysts in a wide range of water bodies such as recreational lakes, in raw river water, sewage and even – most importantly – supposedly treated tap water. Says Tucker: 'It has taken several large disease incidents and the looming twin threats of Mrs Thatcher's rotting sewers and privatisation of water, to prompt this public health project. But don't think for a moment that this problem will go away with a dose of chlorine. It will not.'

Lead in Water

At the time of writing, it looks as if the European Commission will finally bring pressure to bear on the government for its prolonged breach of safety limits on lead in drinking water in Scotland. The lead in almost every Scottish region fails to conform to the 1985 EEC Directive on water quality. Britain has asked for a five-year delay in carrying out the Directive but it is unlikely that the EEC will agree to this.

According to an EEC report, drinking water supplies in Strathclyde, Lothian, Tayside, Grampian, Central Fife, Highland, and Dumfries and Galloway are in breach of the EEC limit of 50 micrograms of lead per litre. Britain has unilaterally declared a limit of 100 micrograms per litre. A survey undertaken by Friends of the Earth showed that six out of forty-one households or workplace drinking water supplies in Glasgow and Edinburgh contained lead in excess of 50 micrograms per litre. One sample was more than eight times higher than that. FoE is urging the EEC to prosecute Britain saying that such high levels are harming the intelligence of Glasgow's and Scotland's youngsters. It is estimated that around 300,000 people in Scotland are drinking water which is dangerously contaminated with lead.

The Scottish Office disputes both the figures and the risk to health but does admit that seventy-eight water supplies in Scotland were in breach of the European limit. A spokesman for the office told *The Guardian* (11 March 1989) that fifty-eight would be 'improved' by the end of 1989 and work started on the other twenty 'will be completed as soon as possible'. It has been known now for a long time that very low levels of lead in the blood of young children can have measurable effects on their performance in ability and attainments tests, can cause hyperactivity and restlessness. Some experts believe that there is no 'safe' level of exposure to lead and that the government should give householders all over the UK grants to remove any existing lead fittings in their water systems.

Nitrates

Our refusal to adhere to EC limits and our way of changing the rules might well prove to be the Achilles' heel of the whole water privatisation programme, because it is the one which leaves us most open to prosecution from Brussels.

Artificial nitrates have been used in unprecedented amounts in recent years to improve the yield of land – with the effect that huge mountains of grain are currently being stored in storage facilities. Concern has been growing for years over the amount leaching into rivers, ponds, ground water and, eventually, into tap water. In 1988, a secret report by scientists from the Water Authorities and Department of the Environment was widely leaked. It identified ten areas of particular risk, four in East Anglia, four in the Midlands, one in Kent and one in Gloucestershire.

It said that in some areas *all* arable farming would have to cease for decades for the soil to become nitrate-free. In some areas, such as North Norfolk, Anglian Water will have to control nitrate pollution of drinking water by further chemical treatment. In other areas of East Anglia the Water Authority blends nitrate-polluted water with water from other areas which is not so heavily contaminated. Anglian Water told the *Sunday Times* (5 March 1989) that it estimated it would cost £90m to clean the nitrates out of its present water supply. But even if it does so, the amount going into it will continue to rise because even if farmers could finally be persuaded to stop using nitrogen fertilisers nitrates will seep through for a further five to forty years. This could mean that rivers like the Great Ouse and Thames which are now within EC limits will exceed them by the end of the century. To show just how little these concerns have got through to farmers, it should be noted that in 1986 1.3m tonnes of nitrogen were being used nationally in fertiliser, twice the figure for 1966.

Nitrates in water have been linked to stomach and intestinal cancers and the blue baby disease methaemoglobinaemia. In this illness the nitrate reacts with bacteria in the gut, depleting blood oxygen levels which then affect the brain and heart muscles.

In 1980, the European Commission ruled that drinking water must not contain more than 50 milligrams of nitrate per litre. In 1984, the World Health Organisation produced evidence of clear links between nitrates and the blue baby syndrome. The EC has pointed to fifty-two areas of Britain with concentrations of nitrates higher than permitted levels and even the government has now admitted that as many as 1.3 million people could be affected. Mothers of small babies are actually advised in some areas – such as parts of East Anglia – not to give their babies tap water even if it is boiled for boiling does not remove nitrates. Some families are now having to spend, literally, hundreds of pounds a year on bottled water. Two years ago Friends of the Earth reported the government to the European Commission for wilful misinterpretations of the agreed limits. Andrew Lees of that body thinks that the government should set up water protection zones where the use of nitrates would be restricted or forbidden and that artificial fertilisers should have a tax put on them of 10 to 15 per cent to cover the cost of dealing with the pollution they cause. As it is, farmland is not even rated so that it is the consumer that pays the polluters' bills.

Pesticides

Like nitrates, pesticides also have a long lifespan – but a virtually unlimited spread – for instance, DDT, now banned, has been found in the breast milk of Eskimo women . . . We have still not obeyed the 1979 Directive to stop selling and using the particularly worrying organo-chlorine pesticides although we are now told they will be forbidden by 1992. The Water Authorities maintain that stringent testing prevents high levels of pesticide residues actually reaching tap water, but not every pesticide can be easily detected in water and some may be toxic even at very low concentrations – such as the herbicide 245T and its dioxin. Again, the heavy usage of pesticides has contributed to the huge food surpluses. They are frequently used in a way for which they were never intended, often in far larger quantities than specified (known as 'insurance' spraying). By the time some crops are harvested they can have been sprayed anything up to ten times with a variety of insecticides and fungicides while the ground around them has been drenched in herbicides.

The Friends of the Earth report on *Pesticides in Drinking Water* does show, as has been discussed elsewhere, just how widespread pesticide contamination of drinking water now is. As the report says:

The results presented significantly understate the scale of the problem. This is because the UK Government's current advice ensures that the majority of water suppliers do not frequently test drinking water for low levels of many pesticides, let alone the other toxic components of pesticide formulations, their 'break-down' products, or the toxic substances formed during the treatment of water which is contaminated by certain pesticides.

The ability of water suppliers to assess compliance with the Maximum Admissible Concentrations (MACs) stipulated in the EC 1985 Directive for pesticides in drinking water is undermined by a shortage of suitable analytical techniques and the high cost of assessing compliance with the MACs using some of the techniques which are available. Furthermore few, if any, water suppliers sample surface water sources often enough to assess seasonal variations in pesticide levels. Thus, many of them have hardly begun to assess compliance with the MACs for pesticides in drinking water.

There is also a paucity of reliable data about the risks of water pollution by many pesticides; a risk which has been greatly under-estimated because successive British governments approved the use of pesticides without taking sufficient account of the high leaching rates from the light, sandy, soils which overlie many of our vulnerable ground water resources or the persistence of pesticides in ground water. Ignorance of the possible health risks due to long-term exposure to low levels of pesticides and the other ingredients in the drinking water 'cocktail', is compounded by serious defects in the safety tests, and gaps in safety test data, for many older pesticides.

These deficiencies and uncertainties mean that the government has no reliable information about the full extent of pesticide contamination in drinking water, let alone the concentrations present and cannot properly assess health hazards.

Between July 1985 and June 1987 the MAC for any single pesticide as specified in the Drinking Water Directive was exceeded in 298 of the water sources and supplies tested by Friends of the Earth. Breaches of the MAC for total pesticides were recorded on seventy-six occasions. Sixteen pesticides were each detected in drinking water supplies at levels above the MAC for a single pesticide, the most common of which were Atrazine and Simazine. The present government has continually pressed the EC to draft an amendment to its Drinking Water Directive which would replace MACs with limits for individual pesticides 'which are more closely related to health risk'. The EC has refused.

Chemicals

According to the report *Assessment of Groundwater* published by the Department of the Environment, in December 1988, many of the country's underground water reserves – which supply about a third of our drinking water – suffer from chemical pollution. The report concludes that 'groundwater is generally good but problems associated with contamination are increasing and its value as a considerably less expensive alternative to surface water is seriously threatened'.

Scientists apparently told those undertaking the survey that the problem is likely to become more severe and that the British have been too complacent about the difficulties it poses. Commenting on the report, *The Independent* (8 December 1988) said that the peculiar difficulty of this type of contamination is that it only provides a 'snapshot' of what was dumped on the surface above it ten years or so previously, so no one knows how much worse it will become as it seeps into water supplies. This has obvious problems for privatisation as the new private companies would be unable to sue the companies who contaminated the water supply as they would be unlikely ever to be able to identify them.

The kind of chemicals which leach into ground water include industrial solvents, commonly used in the chemical, leather, car and dry cleaning industries. In 1983, there was a huge leak of chemical solvent at the US Airforce base at Mildenhall, in Suffolk, which contaminated local ground water, but no charges could be brought because military bases are immune from prosecution for pollution offences.

Aluminium

Aluminium can occur naturally in water but it is also used in purification processes although most of it should be removed from the water before it reaches your tap. It dissolves easily in acidic water of which we now have plenty, thanks to acid rain. Surveys have shown that aluminium levels exceeding the EEC Drinking Water Directive Limit affect over 2 million people in this country. The government's answer has been to seek, as late as June 1988, 'derogations' from the EEC Directives for forty-seven areas of England where the aluminium content is too high.

The forty-seven areas include districts covered by the Northumbrian Water Authority, Severn Trent (including Coventry, Nuneaton, Hinkley and Bosworth), very large areas of the South West Water Authority including most of Cornwall and large parts of Devon, towns such as Stockport and Oldham in the North West Water Authority and large parts of the area covered by Yorkshire Water.

There is now, according to *The Lancet* (14 January 1989), a strong, but so far unproven, link between aluminium in the water and Alzheimer's disease, the onset of early senile dementia which is a growing problem in this country. A survey of eighty-eight county districts in England and Wales showed that the risk of Alzheimer's was 1.5 times higher in districts where the mean aluminium concentrations exceeded 0.11 milligram per litre than in districts where concentrations were less than 0.01 mg/l. That means that cases of Alzheimer's in areas with high aluminium levels in tap water were up 50 per cent on those where it was less. The report in *The Lancet* rightly advises caution in interpreting the data but that, along with other research carried out elsewhere, does suggest that there might well be a problem and that the current levels considered 'safe' might well have to be lowered.

The foregoing shows just what a huge task is now facing us. Massive lack of investment, coupled with complacency, has brought about the situation which now exists and it beggars belief to think that privatised companies will be able to clean up our drinking water, let alone everything else, while, on top of that, paying out vast amounts of extra money for research and development – not to mention, of course, shareholders' profits, flotation costs and huge directors' salaries.

The place of the European Commission in the scheme of things and the adverse legislation now piling up against the UK will be considered in Part II of this book, which deals with the issue of privatisation. In the event, action by the EC could be our only hope. For we have many choices as to what we eat and drink – we can stop eating eggs if salmonella worries us, eat only hard cheese for fear of listeria, forego fatty foods for health reasons, stop smoking or never start, as we know that really does cause horrendous health problems – but we can't stop drinking or using water.

The Lowermoor Incident

There can be no better end to this chapter than to detail the history of what happened – and is still happening – in North Cornwall following the major pollution of a drinking water supply. South West Water Authority, like the other nine, has been gearing up for privatisation. Following government intervention, local authority representatives and other elected officers can no longer sit on Water Authority boards, nor are the press and public allowed into Authority meetings. This is of particular importance when considering the Lowermoor incident.

The SWWA, like all the others, also had to shape itself up to become profitable and, as a result, a price was put on safety. It had been known for some time that keys to locks on equipment, tanks, etc. at water plants were freely available to private contractors, and although a new £100,000 security system was designated for the Camelford area it was decided this should be phased in over ten years in order to save money – according to a leaked Report detailed on *Panorama* on 20 March 1989.

The story, basically, is this. On 6 July 1988, a tanker driver arrived at the Lowermoor water treatment works in North Cornwall. The works, largely automatic, were unmanned and the driver was a relief driver for a chemical firm, unfamiliar with the layout of the works. He was carrying a load of aluminium sulphate to be used as a water purifier. It was not labelled as a hazardous substance. He had received only an oral briefing and been given a key by a regular driver. The key fitted any tank in any of the waterworks and the regular driver had it because it had, in the past, been left hidden for him so that no one need be there when he arrived and he had hung on to it, meaning to return it at some time. The relief driver dumped his load into what he thought was the right tank then pushed an unsigned delivery note under the office door and left – there was, of course, no supervisor around.

It was not the right tank. He had dumped 20 tons of aluminium sulphate into the purified water tank on its way to the mains supply. The result affected 7,000 households and 20,000 people in the Camelford area. As the discoloured water poured out of their taps people began to call South West Water to find out what had happened. They were told there was nothing wrong, it was quite fit to drink, so they did so. They developed sickness, diarrhoea, mouth and nose ulcers, blistered tongues, bloody urine, aches and pains in the muscles, and those already suffering from arthritis found themselves in excruciating agony. For hours officials at South West Water flatly refused to believe there was a problem and a mother who rang and asked if it was safe to use the water for her baby's bottle was told it was. She did so and the baby developed mouth ulcers. Local GP Dr Richard Newman found his surgery flooded with patients presenting with a wide range of distressing symptoms. South West

Water remained silent. On 7 July, 30,000 fish were found dead in the Camel and Allen rivers. South West Water blamed an equipment failure.

On 11 July, Douglas Cross, a biologist and expert on water pollution who actually lives in the area, complained of kidney pains and contacted South West Water. His complaint was rejected.

In fact SWWA had known about the aluminium sulphate in the tank since 8 July and by the time Douglas Cross rang in and the full implications of what had happened had become clear, there is no doubt that SWWA should have warned the entire population of the area and provided an alternative water supply. They did nothing. A somewhat controversial report on the incident written by Dr John Lawrence – controversial because although he was asked to investigate the incident for SWWA he is a board member himself – said that there seemed to be 'a culture in which the public are told as little as possible and were expected to trust the Authority to look after their interests'. The water continued flowing through the taps.

Acidity and alkalinity in water are measured on a continuous scale by a property known as 'pH'. Acids have a low pH and alkalis a high one. It is measured on scales 1–14 and a good water supply should average around 7. Aluminium sulphate is an acid. On the day realisation had finally dawned on SWWA, they did inform the head of community medicine in Cornwall, Dr. Grainger, that there were low pH levels in local water and also elevated aluminium levels – nothing more. On 12 July, he was told of aluminium levels as high as 4 mg/l peaking to 40 mg/l, but since he had received no complaints he took no positive action. Any public queries were still met with the response that the water was safe to drink.

The district manager of SWWA, later sacked, said in a sworn statement that he had been aware as early as 8 July of the possible contamination and that the cause was confirmed on 12 July, but he was told that, 'I must treat this information as strictly confidential and not tell anyone not already aware of the cause.'

On 20 July, the regional operations engineer thought a press release should be issued giving the cause of the incident but this had to be cleared by the chairman and chief executive, Keith Court. A meeting was held to discuss this and the idea was vetoed by Mr Court. Instead it was decided to advertise in the press.

On 22 July – sixteen days after the incident – a small advertisement was placed in one issue of the *Western Morning News* on the sports page. Addressed to residents in the Camelford area, it assured them that their water supply was fit to use and drink. Aluminium had found its way into the water but it was 'no more acidic than lemon juice and was further diluted many times'. This remarkable statement was the *first* public admission that there had been any incident at all.

Meanwhile, people continued to be ill, including one young man who had been involved in an accident and found his wound reopened. It bled for a month.

The long-term implications do not just apply to the aluminium sulphate contamination but to the fact that the water which contained it in its extremely caustic condition caused leaching from water pipes. This has meant that copper, lead and even zinc also leached into the water supply and were taken into the systems of those who drank it. They drank a cocktail of metal-contaminated water.

The reason those with arthritis suffered so badly is that aluminium does not just leach metal out of pipes, it does the same for calcium in bones. There are obvious implications in the long term, especially for women who are particularly vulnerable to osteoporosis (bone loss).

Calls for a public inquiry and the resignation of Keith Court grew in strength but Mr Court made it crystal clear that he saw no reason why he should resign. Nor has the government agreed to a public inquiry. Calls for a full health survey fell on deaf ears for a considerable time although residents in the area have now been asked to fill in a survey form detailing the effects of the water on their health.

In December 1988, water officials admitted that the amount of pollution suffered by the people had been grossly underestimated. Analysis of water samples carried out by independent experts shortly after the incident found that the water had been contaminated by a staggering *6,000 times* the maximum levels considered safe by the EEC and WHO. Original figures showed that water samples contained 620 milligrams per litre of aluminium – 3,100 times the EEC safety limit, but South West Water has now accepted that the real figure was approximately *1,200 milligrams per litre*. The new figures came from samples collected by Douglas Cross who said he had made them available immediately after the accident but had been ignored.

Early in 1989, the government sent down health experts to look into the Camelford incident – they visited the area for a matter of only hours.

By March 1989, reports were coming in of calves being born at only half the normal weight, breeding rabbits becoming sterile and piglets born with both male and female sex organs. Many of those who suffered symptoms back in July were still suffering from them and were also afflicted with chronic tiredness. Forgetfulness and lack of concentration fuel fears of increased Alzheimer's disease. One woman, interviewed by *Panorama* on 20 March explained what had happened to her. She had lived in the area all her life and visited Plymouth regularly. 'I got in my car to drive to Plymouth and suddenly I didn't know the way, I couldn't think of the route.' She said she was frightened as she kept forgetting things. 'The other day I went to put the dinner into the freezer instead of the cooker'.

Mr Court has still not resigned. He is all set to become the chairman of the new privatised water company.

8

Acid Rain

Attending the government-sponsored Ozone Conference in March 1989 and listening to the Prime Minister's speeches was quite an experience. Not only did she go on about the ozone layer (omitting all mention of how we had dragged our feet about agreeing to reduce limits), but she spoke movingly about the greenhouse effect and acid rain as well.

In this country, our principal contributor to acid rain has been power stations burning fossil fuels and the emissions have risen steadily since the turn of the century. But, as is noted in the Greenpeace report on air pollution (1988), written by Andrew Tickle of the Centre for Environmental Technology, Imperial College: 'In spite of the warning signs from Scandinavia and the fact that the potential link between acid deposition and acid waters in the UK had been identified some twenty years previously, recognition of acidification problems has been slow.'

Scotland is particularly affected, especially upland Scotland. The first studies covered the Loch Ard area in the Trossachs where high levels of sulphur were found. In forested areas there was more acid and streams contained higher concentrations of the metals manganese and aluminium. Further work showed, according to Dr Tickle, that 'trees collect air pollutants, giving rise to increased stream concentrations of acidity'. It was probably research in Scotland which, he says, 'together with mounting evidence of loss of fish stocks led to the decision in 1986 by the Central Electricity Generating Board (CEGB) to fit three large UK power stations with flue gas desulphurisation technology in an attempt to control acid emissions. This action was intended to reduce the emissions by 30 per cent by the year 2000.'

The problem is now widespread in the North and West of the country, although parts of Wales and the Cornwall and Devon peninsula are also affected.

The pH factor in water has already been mentioned with regard to the Lowermoor incident and this has also been used to measure acidity in standing water such as lakes. Surveys have shown that there has been a steady decline in pH since industrial times, often accompanied by losses or decline of fish stocks. Measuring the effect on water is, however, far from easy but a working group reporting to the DoE Acid Waters Review Group, in 1986, identified roughly a third of the waters for which good records were available as being vulnerable to acidification.

Dr Tickle writes:

Acidification of surface waters has now been demonstrated unequivocally in Britain and over a far wider area of the country than was hitherto thought. Incontrovertible palaeo-ecological proof from almost all the areas of upland Britain has in particular underlined the extent and, more importantly, the recent (post-1850) timescale of acidification. It is probably this advance in understanding, together with mounting evidence of loss from fish stocks, that has led to the decision by the CEGB to invest in pollution control measures.

However, the extent to which these reductions will influence the pH of surface waters is a key question. Although encouraging signs have been observed that effects may be reversible in some areas this will probably not be the case for all systems. Modelling studies in particular point to the fact that current emissions plans are insufficient to halt, let alone reverse acidification in many areas.

Acid water is now a widespread phenomenon in this country and the acid emissions are the major cause of it along with the decline in fish populations. 'Additional scavenging of acidity from the atmosphere by conifers has also exacerbated the problem in many upland areas.'

All that seems fairly straightforward. We know that fossil fuel power stations contribute to both the greenhouse effect and to acid rain. It is quite possible for filters to be fitted to prevent this from happening – at a price. After many years of not wanting to know, the CEGB was finally getting round to cleaning up its act. The Prime Minister assured us at the Ozone Conference that she was right behind them. But something, somewhere seems to have gone amiss.

In fact we learn from a report in *The Observer* (19 March 1989) that massively *increased* emissions of the gases that cause the above effects are being planned by the CEGB, because the irresistible force has met the immovable object – the two kingsize privatisation programmes have run slap into each other, electricity and water.

The government has resisted all attempts to amend the electricity privatisation bill to force the industry to cut down the pollution which is at the root of the trouble, and energy ministers have agreed to allow the CEGB to delay action to curb it. (Mrs Thatcher said at the Ozone Conference that cutting back on pollution was 'crucial' . . .)

She, however, boycotted the heavier weight conference in The Hague the following week when twenty-four world leaders said that the heating up of the earth's atmosphere threatened the very conditions of life on the planet. The CEGB is, in answer to this threat, proposing to increase its annual emissions of carbon dioxide by 45 million tons a year – 25 per cent – over the next fifteen years. The board has told the government that cleaning up the act would cause problems and would not be consistent with the continued achievement of reasonable rates of growth in the country. A delay of a decade would not, it says, 'make a great deal of difference'.

In fact junior Energy Minister Baroness Hooper has said that the government will not be 'panicked' into taking measures, nor has it allowed amendments to the Electricity Privatisation Bill which included the provision that the new companies would not be allowed to build new power stations if they could save the amount of energy more cheaply through conservation. (Similar provisions, writes *The Observer*'s environment correspondent, Geoffrey Lean, have proved enormously successful in the USA and Norway.)

On top of all this, the country's energy conservation programme is being run down: the budget of the Energy Efficiency Office is being cut by half; the government has scrapped home insulation grants except in special cases; it has closed a programme which spends £7m a year financing pilot projects to demonstrate energy savings; it is opposing an EEC Directive to provide housebuyers with information on the energy costs of their homes; and it has voted down thirty amendments introducing conservation measures into the Electricity Privatisation Bill.

So never mind the talk, watch the action. The power stations will continue to pump out pollution which will cause both acid rain to fall into our – and other people's – streams, rivers and lakes while at the same time accelerating the greenhouse effect.

It is clear from the preceding chapters that our waterways, lakes, sewers, beaches and tap water are in a dire state. This is the result of years of neglect by successive governments and virtually total neglect during the last ten years by this one. With the privatisation of water always in their sights, this government has deliberately forced the Water Authorities to make getting themselves ready for it their priority, before anything else.

It would take enormous sums of money to put matters right but then we do have 'loadsamoney', much of it from the sale of other national assets. Opinion polls show that the majority of the population would like to see their tax money spent on repairing sewers and cleaning up water. It is not, as the Chancellor would have it, even inflationary to do so.

But common sense and public good must not, it seems, stand in the way of political dogma however foolish and ill-considered. The second half of this book deals with the many different aspects of privatisation and how it will affect every household in Britain – together with what the European Commission might do to put a spanner in the works.

PART II

Privatisation

9

The Run-up to the Sell Out

Preparations for selling off water to private companies began in the early 1980s. One of the main planks of the government's proposal for the sale is that the quality of water and service will need private capital to bring it up to the standards consumers want. It is true that both standard and service, as we have seen, *is* inadequate but many of the reasons for this can be laid directly at the door of the government itself. What it has done during the run-up to privatisation has directly contributed to the state of the industry. As NALGO says: 'Once the reasons for any failings in the service are examined it is clear how cynical the government can be when it deals with essential public services.'

A two-pronged attack was mounted on the water industry. First, came the setting of swingeing financial targets in 1981 followed by a variety of operational reforms under the 1983 Water Act. The financial constraints were imposed to lower the amount of outstanding debt owed by the Water Authorities and to make them more like the private companies they were to become – leaner, more efficient and, above all, profitable.

The maximum amount of annual capital expenditure was lowered and even tighter limits set on borrowing. The authorities were set arbitrary and artificial profit targets and were expected to meet them. Similarly, they were set arbitrary performance aims.

I am indebted to NALGO for the details of how all this breaks down. Cuts in annual expenditure have been growing steadily since 1979 with, as NALGO explains, 'only occasional exceptions where authorities have convinced the government that only a slight increase would prevent catastrophe'.

Using the powers invested in it by the 1973 Water Act, the government has made cuts which have been compounded by the decline of what is known as the 'external financial limit'. This sets the amount of money the water authorities can borrow, which in turn limits the extent to which capital financial requirements can be financed by external borrowing, leasing or government grants, which then reduces the amount of money Water Authorities can borrow to undertake capital projects – such as major sewer repairs.

So the only way the authorities have been able to increase their revenue is through higher water rates and charges. In 1975, 80 per cent of the Water Authorities' expenditure was financed by borrowing. Today, that figures is less than 10 per cent. The government calls this 'good housekeeping' but no private industry could act in this way. Private industry borrows money so that expenditure on major capital investment can be spread over a period of years. The excuse cannot even be used that money would be borrowed for short-term gains. The reservoirs, sewers, and water treatment plants are not like cars – they are assets which last for generations.

So, currently, consumers are paying not only the full cost of running the water industry but for future expenditure as well. At the same time, the authorities are supposed to be using money to clear their debts ready for the big bang.

Like everything else from the London Underground (with what result!) to electricity, the water industry must be seen to be profitable so arbitrary targets were set. Just like those at London Underground Limited, the managers of the Water Authorities have enthusiastically leapt to do what they are told and they now consistently average above their profit targets. The industry's rate of return has risen from 1.0 per cent in 1984–5 to 1.6 per cent in 1986–7 with some authorities like Thames now self-financing. This has been achieved by massive underinvestment, cuts in staffing levels and the contribution of the consumer.

To help it all along the industry has been made to switch from historical cost accounting to current accounting, a convention very rarely used in private industry. The effect of the current cost method is to make the profits of nationalised industries look smaller than they actually are and the result for the water industry, along with the financial targets, has been to make the targets for profit much higher.

Performance aims have also been set for the industry for both sewage and water supply. These are not, let it be emphasised, targets for the *services* provided but financial targets (again) which have led to direct cuts in service and the state of our rivers, sewers, water treatment plants and tapwater. According to NALGO over 13,000 jobs, 20 per cent of the total for the industry, have been lost since 1979.

But this was not all. In 1983, came yet another reorganisation of the industry under the new Water Act. This was entirely designed to make the authorities as much like private companies as possible and establish commercialism as the core and ideal. With all the drum beating about consumers having more freedom and there being more personal choice, this piece of legislation was directly designed to do away with the concept of public accountability.

To this end, local authority representation on water boards was abolished thus meaning that no one sitting on them had actually been democratically elected and could be held accountable to those electors. Boards were made smaller and the members were directly appointed by central government, dominated by business interests.

The rights of press and public to attend Water Authorities' meetings was abolished. It was decided that all that need happen was for a press release to be issued afterwards if this was felt to be necessary. As has been seen, this particular clause was crucial in the case of the Lowermoor incident for it enabled South West Water to cover up what had actually happened for weeks and for its chairman and chief executive, Keith Court, to veto any suggestions that the real position should be spelled out to the unfortunate consumers. The lack of any local authority representation ensured that the pollution was kept under wraps. Water authority meetings are, therefore, held in secret.

The National Water Council, which had coordinated a nationwide policy for the industry, was also abolished and there has been no national policy for water for the last six years. The water industry was then carved up into the individual Water Authorities which became autonomous bodies.

Perhaps this is the point to mention the water providers which are not part of the still publicly owned big ten. They are the twenty-eight private 'statutory' water companies which provide 28 per cent of the water in England and Wales – the ones who have just dramatically hiked up their prices. These companies are used to point out that private companies can operate just as well, if not better, than publicly owned Water Authorities.

Currently, they are 'statutory companies', that is, they have to operate within strict limits laid down by legislation. Their responsibilities, as NALGO points out, are constitutionally linked to the Water Authorities and there are financial controls written into their statutes. These put a top limit on the rate of their dividends, the size of their reserves and the balance that can be carried forward from one year to the next. Furthermore, unlike the Water Authorities, they have no responsibility for sewage. Their role is only to supply water.

Their survival was preserved by another Conservative government Water Act back in 1974, which allowed them to remain in business by forcing the Water Authorities in which they were situated to provide some of the supplies in their areas through these companies. However, the terms of their relationship with the Water Authorities were set firmly under Water Authority control through integrated river basin management.

Writing in *The Economist*, in September 1987, Jack Jeffrey, chairman of the Water Companies Association, admitted that the present private companies are not at all like the private companies envisaged under privatisation. 'We are subject to strict financial controls especially on dividends which make us very different from the WSPLCs being proposed.'

Under privatisation the links between the statutory water

companies and the Water Authorities will be severed and controls over them lifted. They would become ordinary public liability companies just like the newly privatised Water Authorities and would share the same statutes. Like them, they would be ripe for take-over or it could be the other way around.

It is not surprising that our water industry is becoming a tasty morsel for outside speculators. During the run-up period outside companies, especially the French, have been buying into the private water companies. French owned companies currently have stakes in sixteen of the private companies whose share values have increased 40 per cent since 1987.

Perhaps it would be informative to finish this chapter with a table of who has bought shares in what – to which I am again indebted to NALGO.

'Water Fund' is a recently formed company established by Southern Water and Associated Insurance Pension Fund (AIPF). The list does not include Bournemouth and District, Chester, Cholderton and District, Hartlepool, Sutton District, Wrexham and East Denbighshire, and York for which information is not available.

Cementation–SAUR is a company formed by a UK subsidiary of Générale des Eaux, General Utility and Trafalgar House. Lyonnaise des Eaux has a longstanding relationship with John Laing, the UK construction company. Both Northumbria Water and Southern Water actually bought into their local statutory water companies but the former sold out after the water industry unions began court action to test whether this was legal. At the time of writing, proceedings were still pending against Southern Water.

But note the buy-ins from Générale des Eaux, Lyonnaise des Eaux, Cementation–SAUR and Bouygues – not to mention the buy-out of Newcastle and Gateshead and Sunderland and South Shields. There is nothing to stop the French eventually buying up the entire British water industry after privatisation. What does this patriotic government want us to do about it – sing 'Rule Britannia' in unison?

Company	Stakeholder	Percentage
Bristol	Lyonnaise des Eaux	18
	Générale des Eaux	30
Cambridge	Cambs. Water Emp. Invst. Club	18
Colne Valley	Générale des Eaux	28
	Cementation–SAUR	24
East Anglian	Lyonnaise des Eaux	45
Essex	Lyonnaise des Eaux	*98*
Eastbourne	Equity & Law	29
	AIPF/Southern Water Fund	35
Folkestone & District	AIPF	10
	Unknown stake of Bouygues	
Mid Kent	Morgan Grenfell	27
	Générale des Eaux	23
	AIPF	2
Lee Valley	Générale des Eaux	23
	Cementation–SAUR	15
Newcastle & Gateshead	Générale des Eaux	£30.5m agreed bid
Portsmouth	Employment Retirement Benefit Scheme	84
Rickmansworth	Cementation–SAUR	28
Mid Southern	Générale des Eaux	14
	Current bid by Bouygues	
South Staffs	Générale des Eaux	24
East Surrey	AIPF	28
North Surrey	Générale des Eaux	20
	Cementation–SAUR	15
Mid Sussex	AIPF/Southern Water/Water Fund	32
	Bid by Bouygues	
Sunderland & South Shields	Lyonnaise des Eaux	£29.8m agreed bid
Tendring Hundred	Générale des Eaux	16
West Hampshire	Unknown Biwater stake	
East Worcester	Biwater Supply	62
	Royal Trust Asset Mngt	12
West Kent	AIPF	30
	Southern Water	15
	Bouygues	16+

10

The Need for Capital Expenditure

As we have seen, the growing amount of pollution in our waters coupled with the severe restraints which have been placed on the Water Authorities, curbing expenditure on the infrastructure, means that it will now take a great deal of money to maintain the status quo let alone improve matters.

Many water mains are reaching the end of their natural lives. Water continually seeps from leaking and corroded pipes, on top of which there are major bursts. It is estimated that about one-third of the water going into the mains pipes of that flagship, the Thames Water Authority, actually *never reaches the taps*, so poor is the condition of the 80-year-old pipes which carry much of it. This is not even the worst authority. North West Water is estimated to lose *half* its water in this way. It is difficult to conceive of any other industry allowing its resource literally to drain away in so profligate a manner.

Burst water mains do not just lose water either. NALGO, in its paper on the subject, describes how in July 1987 a burst water main in central London actually stopped the Northern and Victoria underground lines for two days. Bus queues swelled, traffic came to a halt and thousands of commuters were left stranded. The flood caused more than £5m worth of damage to property. Nor was this all. On the very same day, South London also ground to a halt following another mains burst which, in this incident, also cut off gas and water supplies to homes.

As mentioned previously, old lead pipes are a serious cause for concern and we have already run foul of the EEC Directive in this respect. It is not just Scotland which gives rise to anxiety. The chronically overloaded water system of the North West Thames area supplies 600,000 homes through corroded old lead pipes, creating dangerous levels of lead in the drinking water. The Water Authority itself claims that 40 per cent of its mains pipes suffer from unacceptable degrees of corrosion and mineral deposits and 35 per cent of its water is of an unacceptable standard. In the Severn Trent area, old iron pipes are so corroded that blisters reduce their capacity by half, causing rust in water, serious infestation of animals, lower water pressure and, of course, more burst mains.

An enormous amount of money needs to be spent on our sewers, many of which are unmapped. It is estimated that there are 150,000 miles of sewer pipes in the areas of the various Water Authorities of which about 15,000 miles – 10 per cent – are over a hundred years old. As NALGO says: 'As overloading and structural decay worsens, more and more of them are collapsing. According to the Secretary of State for the Environment, in 1986 there were 3,500 collapses and 1,500 blockages requiring excavation.'

It is these old sewers which cause the 'back surges' continually experienced in some areas of Plymouth, for instance, where houseowners find that sewage has flowed back up the pipe and re-entered their homes through their lavatory bowls or up their drains. The same can happen if a back surge happens outside – then sewage floods back into streets.

All areas have problems. The Yorkshire Water Authority has more collapses per mile of sewer than any other and needs considerable investment. It has no idea of the real state of 95 per cent of its sewers – in fact it only knows where 70 per cent of them are. The North West has the highest total number of sewer collapses – about four a day. This authority calculates it also has about 700 'unsatisfactory storm overflows' (which take raw sewage into rivers) – about half the national total.

Thames Water Authority holds first prize for the number of homes flooded with sewage annually, with about four incidents taking place *each day*. Some 13,000 householders experience this at regular intervals.

It is very hard to estimate just how much capital expenditure will be needed. The Water Authorities have estimated that it would cost over a billion pounds to restore the sewer system properly. Even in the early 1970s, before the last ten years of severe financial restraint, a report of a survey concluded that it would take a billion pounds – at that point in time – to provide the investment that was needed for land drainage, flood protection and sea defences.

As to water quality, the Water Authorities themselves believe that a figure of 'some billions of pounds' will be needed to ensure compliance with EEC legislation on water. The Robens Institute, in evidence to the House of Commons Environment Committee, estimated that, to conform merely to the EEC standards for nitrates in drinking water, Anglian Water alone would have to invest £900m, Severn Trent £40m and the Thames Water Authority £40m. These are vast sums. Nor can we look for help from the European Community because they are far less likely to give money for grant aid from the European Regional Development Fund to private industry.

In order to assist the Water Authorities out of these appalling financial difficulties in the run-up to privatisation, the government has kindly invited them to have their pollution standards relaxed. This invitation came in a letter from the Department of the Environment to the Chief Executives of the Water Authorities, a copy of which was given to *The Observer* (1 January 1989). Written just two months after Environment Secretary Nicholas Ridley had assured the House of Commons that the desire to make privatisation a success would not prompt him to relax pollution standards, it actually invited the authorities to contact its own Pollution Inspectorate to see three separate ways of relaxing their pollution limits.

This would enable the Water Authorities to sign the necessary flotation prospectuses which they would not be able to do under the present situation if they are persistently committing criminal offences. Mr Marek Mayer, editor of *Environmental Data Services*, a leading technical pollution journal, told the newspaper that he estimated that at least a third of the country's 6,340 sewage works would be eligible for this new deal.

Meanwhile, immunity from prosecution over environmental pollution is being sought by the Water Authorities once water is privatised. We know this thanks to another leak, this time a briefing note to a group of ten Conservative MPs known as the 'Friends of Water' . . . The note warns that if the water companies are to be able to manage 'successfully and profitably' they should not be open to prosecution or enforcement orders for environmental improvements – providing they can show they are doing all they reasonably can to comply with requirements (*The Independent*, 20 January 1989). The 'Friends of Water' MPs have been especially selected, one to 'represent' each of the ten Water Authorities. Three of them were on the Standing Committee of the Water Bill. It appears that the Water Authorities did not consider verbal assurances, that they would not be prosecuted, sufficient. They wanted this in writing and on the record in Parliament. According to the briefing note, the Authorities feel, 'It is all right for a government Minister speaking on a *Panorama* programme but we would like some written assurances from the government along these lines' (i.e. those of the briefing note).

Just what privatisation is really going to cost will be looked at in more detail in a later chapter but the picture is already becoming clear – all this capital expenditure which is so badly needed, all the cleaning up, all of it, in fact will be paid for – by you!

11

The Water Bill

The Department of Energy summarised the main purposes of the Water Bill in a news release on 24 November 1988. It was:

- to establish a new public body, the National Rivers Authority, to take over the responsibilities of Water Authorities in England and Wales in relation to water pollution, water resource management, flood defence, fisheries, recreation and navigation;
- to provide for the appointment of a Director General of Water Services to keep under review the provision of water and sewerage services and to protect the interests of consumers of those services;
- to establish a new statutory framework for the control of drinking water quality, river quality and other standards; for example, the Secretary of State will set new objectives for river quality, and the National River Authority will be required to control polluting discharges and to take other steps in order to attain these objectives;
- and otherwise to amend and update the law relating to water supply, sewerage services, water pollution, the management of water resources, flood defence and fisheries;
- to provide for terms of appointment and financial arrangements for new limited companies to provide water and sewerage services in England and Wales; the existing statutory

water companies will be appointed to continue to provide water supply in their areas;
- to provide for the transfer of the property, rights and assets of the Water Authorities to the successor water and sewerage companies and the National Rivers Authority; and
- to provide for the sale of shares of the new companies.

The arguments used by the government to justify this ultimate privatisation are:

1 Efficiency – that private enterprise is *always* more efficient.
2 The consumer will have more freedom as private enterprise can offer a wider provision than can the state.
3 It will bring about wider share ownership – that true public ownership will be developed by selling assets to the public.

Some 20 million households, workplaces, etc. a day are supplied by the Water Authorities and statutory companies. As Joint Action for Water Services (JAWS) puts it:

> The entire cycle from rainfall to discharge into the sea is overseen by the ten main authorities. They gather, purify and pipe 13 million litres a day, then drain, treat and get rid of the results (including 2,500 tonnes a day, dry weight, of sludge). They employ some 50,000 people to do it. Their joint turnover is £2.7bn a year, their capital spending £1.1 billion, their historic cost operating profit is £1.1bn. Turnover of this size, when coupled with the industry's net current cost assets – in excess of £27bn – make an attractive proposition for Government and Treasury.

Initially, the government had decided that all that required to be done was to convert the existing Water Authorities into ten new Water Service Public Liability Companies (WSPLCs), transferring them to the private sector exactly as they are now. There followed an outcry at this first proposal after which the Department of the Environment backed off a little and it was announced that there would be a National Rivers Authority.

So under the bill as it stands – and every single amendment has been bitterly fought and defeated – only the utility functions of water supply, sewerage, sewage treatment and disposal will be transferred to the private sector. The public sector will retain water conservation and resource planning, pollution control, land drainage, flood protection and navigation. These come under the auspices of the NRA.

As well as the NRA, there will be a separate regulatory authority to control prices and responses to emergencies to be known as OFWAT (Office of Water Supply) and this would be modelled on OFTEL and OFGAS (and we all know how effective they are!). Local consumer consultative committees will be wound up and replaced with Customer Service Committees (CSCs) on which local authorities would not have any representation and which would have no staff of their own.

'The central issue, however,' says NALGO, 'is the NRA and its relationship with WSPLCs. The extent of the NRA's jurisdiction, and its legal authority to regulate the WSPLCs within those areas, are both uncertain, as is its relationship with HM Inspectorate of Pollution, which was set up in April 1987, only a month before plans for the NRA were announced.' Each NRA will have ten to twelve members – two appointed by the Minister of Agriculture and Fisheries (MAFF), one by the Secretary of State for the Environment. Democracy does not enter into it as none of the board members will be elected.'

The NRA will have operational and management functions as well as regulatory ones which means dividing the responsibility for the water cycle between a national body and a series of privatised water companies. This in turn will bring about the abandonment of integrated river basin management.

Integrated river basin management has, hitherto, been accepted on all sides as the best way to manage water. When accepting privatisation back in 1985, the Water Authorities Association said that this assent was conditional on the geographical form and administrative functions of the authorities being kept intact as they believed implicitly in integrated river basin management. So, at that stage apparently, did the government. For in its original White Paper it said: 'The principle of integrated river basin management – a single body controlling water sewerage in each river catchment – has worked well since it was introduced by the Water Act 1973 and will be retained.' And: 'The catchment-based structure of the water industry has worked well in practice. It has been recognised throughout the world as being a good and cost effective model for other countries to follow. It is the main reason why the Government intends to retain the structure of the water authorities essentially as they stand in the transfer to private ownership.'

At present, this system works so that water is organised according to the contours of the land, which forms a natural planning unit. It has meant that the different specialists concerned with providing drinkable water and treating sewage have been able to function together in a single unit, thus making the system more efficient and cost effective. The specialists work together as a team.

Under the Water Bill, the operational management and regulatory functions will be divided between the NRA and the new WSPLCs. There cannot any longer be any true integrated river basin management – even though the government itself described this form of management as a 'good and cost effective model for other countries to follow'.

JAWS, in a paper published in October 1988, estimated that the cost of the new NRA would be in the region of £33.4m – for which the taxpayer would pick up the bill. However, the water industry disputed this, putting the figure at nearer £350m.

In its desire to get the legislation through, the government seems to be saying that the NRA will be all things to all men, which is manifestly impossible. It assures the environmental lobby, on the one hand, that it will have sufficient powers and resources to be able to deal comprehensively and efficiently with the enormous environmental problems involved (which, as NALGO points out, would imply very tight quality and performance regulation of WSPLCs), while at the same time assuring the City and the prospective private water companies that the NRA will not in any way impede the freedom of operation of the new companies.

The government has got itself into a double bind situation

here. Its own chief adviser on privatised industries, Professor Stephen Littlechild, has already pointed out that the more targets the government sets, and the higher the standards, the less attractive the flotation becomes and the less will be realised on that flotation.

Virtually everyone expects the environmentalists to lose out to the City. Already the mechanism is there to draw the teeth of the NRA with suggestions that operational responsibility for it might well be contracted back to the newly privatised companies or put out to private tender to other companies, whether they had experience of the water industry or not.

The new NRA will be the body responsible for issuing those consents which have proved so unsuccessful and so contentious. Even if it is not contracted out, it will be expected to be a slimline operation although there is dispute as to how many people it will employ to carry out its work. So what will it do about the standards of sewage emissions and the various consents, including industrial consents?

This is where the invitation to Water Authorities to relax their rules comes in, so that standards will have already been lowered before the NRA takes over. It would not do for the new body to start demanding the replacement or renewal of existing plants or that all such plants be brought up to higher standards. The prospective private companies have already made it quite clear that they do not see the costs needed for such operations or indeed those necessary to implement all the EC Directives as being their responsibility. If water to EEC standard is wanted and sewage works renewed, then this must come either from general taxation or from vastly increased water charges. It is also made crystal clear that none of this must affect shareholders' profits.

NALGO, which has probably researched the ramifications of the Water Bill more thoroughly than anyone else, looks at the implications of what is proposed. In its report, *Water Down the Drain?*, it gives a few examples of what is to come:

1 Essential research carried out by the Water Research Centre (WRC) – 'rightly described by Environment Secretary Nich-

olas Ridley as a world leader' – will be threatened. After privatisation it will have to compete commercially for contracts; although some of its work can bring rapid commercial results, much of this (such as research into water quality and health) is not so immediately or obviously financially beneficial.

2 'In the Thames region, an £8.5m project to reinstate flows in rivers suffering water depletion' (now recognised as a growing and urgent problem) 'will inevitably be at risk. The purpose of this project is to reverse the damage to flora, fauna and local amenities; it would not be in the interests of the new WSPLCs to continue this work, or to instigate similar projects in the future.'

3 'Under the government's plans, one kind of drainage (through sewer pipes) would be the responsibility of the WSPLCs, while another (from surface water) would be the responsibility of the NRA. However, in many large cities – most notably London – the two are often contained together in a giant pipe called a "storm sewer". Many of these are in a serious state of decay – but the government has not said who will be responsible for repairing them.'

4 'Flood forecasting depends on constant monitoring of hydrological data, at present held by one source alone. After privatisation, WSPLCs would only hold information about their own area; everything else would be held by the NRA. Nobody would have an accurate national *and* local picture and this would be compounded by the fact that only WSPLC staff would be on 24-hour duty. For much of the time they would not be able to obtain information necessary to deal with emergencies, even if it was their responsibility to do so.'

The view of the government is that these conflicting interests can be sorted out but it is difficult to see how this could be, any more than they were in nineteenth-century Birmingham where those of the private water companies were in direct conflict with Joseph Chamberlain's attempts to improve general public health. Bill Stanley, head of corporate strategy at Thames Water, is quoted as saying: 'Once you put activities in the hands of separate bodies they become areas of conflict rather than management.'

Along with the Water Bill came the Public Utilities and Water Charges Bill, the 'Paving Bill' to prepare the way for privatisation. Other Paving Bills have been used by this government for everything from doing away with the Greater London Council to preparing the way for the selling of the nationalised gas industry. It allows the government to spend vast sums on advertising the coming sale and, among other things, has set up trial water metering schemes in different parts of the country.

At this stage, it may be felt that the doubts expressed about the capital expenditure required, the funding and the likely outcome has been weighted on the side of gloom because many of the figures quoted have come from those opposed to water privatisation, such as NALGO and JAWS. However, it is interesting to note that an article in *The Spectator* (1 April 1989) – which may be quirky and idiosyncratic but is not a journal noted for its left-wing tendencies – comes to somewhat similar conclusions.

Entitled *Water, Water Everywhere*, it details the experiences of its author, Edward Whitley, on a trip through some of London's sewers. He says:

> Thames Water is the biggest of the ten water authorities which is to be sold in October. A cursory review of its accounts reveals the depths of the financial quagmire through which the Government is floundering. The current value of Thames Water's assets is £6bn (compared with the £11bn of Britain's largest company, BP) and it makes annual profits of £85m. How can a business which earns a paltry 1.4% returns on its assets be sold on the stock market? The answer, clear as mud to the investing public, is simple to an accountant. Instead of valuing the assets at what they are worth today, put them in the books at their historic cost. Lo and behold, the same assets become worth only £1.4bn and, with the corresponding reduction in depreciation needed to replace them, profits rise to £211m.

> These entirely fictitious figures represent a respectable return of 15 per cent which everybody can understand. So the Government is either giving away £4.6bn of tax-payers' money to the

lucky future shareholders of Thames Water PLC, or it is overstating the profits which these unfortunates will be buying by 150 per cent . . . In the small print of Thames Water's accounts, it is disarmingly revealed that in 1988 68 sewage works (about 17% of the total) 'failed to comply with their consent conditions. These works account for 10 per cent of the total sewage treated'. The value of sewage-related assets comprises perhaps 80 per cent of Thames Water's total assets representing a total worth of £4.8bn. The implications of this sentence – which received slightly less prominence than such sensational events of Thames Water's year as 'it was decided to lift the regulation making it necessary for boardsailers to wear full dry suits at all times' – are that almost £1bn worth of sewage works should not be operating, and that half a million cubic metres of mistreated sewage are being pumped into the River Thames every day.

He then describes how Thames Water stocked the river with 109,000 salmon parr and 35,000 smolts in 1988, believing their own success story as pictured on their posters which show salmon leaping through 'sparkling cascades of silvery water'. Actually, he says, of the 872,000 salmon introduced to the brown waters of the Thames over the last ten years, just 968 have ever been either captured or even reported. He also points out that Thames were notified by third parties of over 3,000 pollution incidents last year and

> the awe and trepidation in which offenders stand of Thames Water can perhaps only be adequately gauged by the fact that there were no less than 32 prosecutions by Thames Water for illegal discharges, an unspecified number of which were successful, and that this regulatory giant – whose area of responsibility reaches from Gravesend to Swindon and Banbury – managed to implement fines amounting to just under £15,000. One can only speculate how this sum might have been increased if Thames Water had brought itself to court.

He then details at repellent length what it was like down Thames Water's sewers. He found a gang of men working on one pile of rubbish with their hands. It had just been discovered that it was the only overflow sewer off the main trunk in that particular area. If the main sewer itself became blocked then 220 million gallons of effluent a day would pour into the already partially blocked one. Whitley asked how long it would take to clear the potential blockage and was told 'about four months'.

His questions to various people at Thames Water had met with little success. He had to send in a list of questions he would like to ask before being granted an interview and all questions which included such inopportune words as 'assets', 'expenditure', 'future', 'privatisation', 'forecast' or 'money' had to be deleted because they were 'price sensitive information' ahead of privatisation.

He finally wades his way out of the effluent considering just what privatisation is going to mean and how worthy an investment Thames Water will be – an organisation which is, apparently, happy to allow gangs of men to move by hand rubbish covered in sewage, which condemns thousands of salmon parr and smolts to certain death in the river, which only imposed fines of £15,000 on 3,000 pollution incidents. But, above all:

> my sense of outrage was reserved for the fact that the management is complacent enough to condone taking four months to clear the only overflow from the trunk sewer to Beckton. If a terrorist were clever enough to plant a bomb anywhere on this trunk sewer, there would be the alluring prospect of 220 million gallons of raw sewage sluicing unstoppably over East London every day with no means of diversion. I can only presume that all the management of Thames Water PLC will live conveniently upstream.

12

Politics – Inside the House and Out

> There be land rats and water rats, land thieves and water thieves . . .
>
> *The Merchant of Venice*

Dr John Cunningham used these words from Shakespeare when the Water Bill came before the House of Commons for its Second Reading on 7 December 1988. It seems they echo what a large proportion of the population feels.

'One thing is clear,' said *The Independent* (4 February 1989), 'the public is agin it. Whatever its views on British Petroleum, Aerospace, Steel, Airports Authority and all, and despite the share bonanza that followed them, the great British public was and remains solidly opposed to, privatising electricity, gas and water.' In an opinion poll taken by NOP in December 1986, 71 per cent of those polled wanted to keep these essential services in state hands. Only 21 per cent were in favour of privatising them. Gas went ahead regardless. Two years later, in December 1988, public hostility to selling off electricity and water remained. A MORI poll showed that 69 per cent opposed selling off electricity with only 23 per cent for it. The ratio for water was even more marked – 75 per cent did not want water to be privatised and only 15 per cent were in favour.

However, such hostility makes no difference to the current

government which can smash its bill through Parliament without fear, owing to its enormous majority. While a number of Conservative MPs have very real reservations about it there will be enough lobby fodder to ensure a famous victory when the vote comes.

Reading through the debate on the bill's Second Reading and its Committee stages is a depressing business. While it may be said with some justification that the opposition parties (and all of them are opposed to it) take a predictable stand and come up with predictable amendments and statements, the response of government is an appalling mixture of arrogance and complacency. There is no effort even to argue the case with passion, putting forward arguments with which one might disagree but would respect. Instead there is page after page of patronising discourse, punctuated with schoolboy jokes, snide comments and poor argument. In fact all argument and response merely reiterates again and again that water privatisation is best, that privatisation is better than public ownership, that all will be well and that anyway, as with the Health Service Review and the privatisation of electricity, it does not matter what arguments are used or what people say or how much they oppose it, it will go through anyway. This is called the democratic process.

To return to Dr Cunningham.

The Bill sets out to create the most far-reaching private monopoly powers ever conceived by a government . . . The Secretary of State lamely excuses private monopoly powers under the Bill by saying that water supply and sewerage disposal will be subject to the disciplines of the private sector – comparative competition, I believe, is the euphemism for that. Everyone in the House knows that such disciplines in the private sector exist only where there is competition. They come from the working of market forces. However, under these proposals there will be no market, no choice and no option. For consumers, no market forces will exist in the supply of domestic tap water or sewerage services.

He then went on to remind the House that when this question had been raised with Mr Ridley earlier, that Minister had wittily responded, 'Let people buy Perrier.'

All the various issues which have either already been covered or will be, in successive chapters, have been rehearsed during both the debate and the Committee stage – pollution, cost, charges and their effects, development of land owned by Water Authorities, the EEC Directives and the effect on the public. On the question of pollution, Sir Hugh Rossi, also speaking on the bill's Second Reading, made his own reservations clear while broadly supporting the idea of water privatisation. He was particularly concerned over apparent loopholes which would make the system of monitoring 'consents' even more difficult.

Speaking of his work on the Select Committee on Environmental Pollution, he quoted the Severn Trent Water Authority as saying: ' It is possible for a discharger to introduce some new contaminant not envisaged when the consent was granted, and hence not limited, to cause serious pollution and then claim this protection. Protection should apply only to those components of the effluent which are governed by specific conditions.'

Sir Hugh continued: 'If an industrial plant is given permission to discharge a chemical into a river, but adds another chemical, it is able to say, "I cannot be prosecuted." As the law stands, it has a licence to discharge, and the fact that the chemical it is discharging is not mentioned in its licence gives it a measure of protection.' He gave a specific example of this of a company discharging cadmium into the River Aire. 'Cadmium is one of the two most poisonous substances known to man, but a company is discharging 12 kilograms of it per annum under a licence which does not refer to it. The Water Authority is unable to prosecute.' The same kind of loophole would apply under clause 101, but clause 100 will make it an offence to permit any poisonous or polluting matter knowingly to enter controlled water. Sir Hugh wanted to know if this would now be tightened up to stop pollutants going into rivers because they are not officially covered by a consent. He suggested a new clause combining clauses 100 and 101.

Sir Hugh's intervention was a rare excursion into the debate by a Conservative MP, most of the talking being left to the opposition. One does not always have to agree with MP Paul Boateng to accept that he had a point when he remarked on the 'bizarre' range of character witnesses 'traipsed before the court as a sign of the worth of the indefensible'. These included Sir Winston Churchill (who would have been for it) and, apparently, according to Mr Dudley Fishburn, MP for Kensington, the late Mahatma Gandhi would also have approved. The somewhat convoluted reason for this being that he had led his people on salt marches to the edge of the sea. As Paul Boateng points out, the marches were to proclaim that the salt belonged to the people and should not be usurped by the state through the imposition of taxation!

The reply to this day's debate came from the Junior Environment Minister, Colin Moynihan, who said he felt that the National Rivers Authority would be able to deal with the question of pollution satisfactorily.

The Committee stage seems to have consisted mostly of vain attempts to persuade the government to agree to various Amendments – something which past governments were reasonably open to – all without success. These ranged from Conservative MP Emma Nicholson's desire that the legislation should give as great a priority to the new PLCs providing fresh, clean water as it does to promoting economy and efficiency, to another which would allow ramblers and hikers the same access to the countryside around reservoirs, rivers and lakes that they currently enjoy.

The happenings in Parliament have been accompanied not so much by leaked information but by a torrent of it. An early harbinger of trouble came with a report in *The Independent* on 7 December 1988, which noted that the twenty-eight statutory water companies were being encouraged by Whitehall to maximise their charges in advance of privatisation. Labour's spokesman on the Water Bill, Ann Taylor, had received a copy of a letter from Ernst Whinney, the chartered accountants advising the private water companies. It said:

The next tariff increase say 1 January or 1 April, is almost certain to be the last opportunity to increase tariffs under the existing regulatory formula prior to the introduction of price cap control. Companies should therefore ensure that the next tariff setting takes *full* account of the consequences of future asset management plans and the costs of these, which we envisage may well mean each company raising its tariffs to the maximum extent permitted under the existing regulatory formula.

It continued: 'Companies are advised not to suggest that privatisation as such makes these tariff increases necessary.' However, ministers did expect that, and had been making official statements to the effect that water undertakings had substantial additional capital expenditure to incur and this would lead to a general increase in tariffs.

When the story broke and much capital was made of it by the opposition parties, the government reaction was that it would not happen and any suggestion that it would was merely 'scaremongering'. To the acute embarrassment of all concerned, at the beginning of February 1989 the private water companies warned that their charges would rise by at least 30 per cent during the coming year – one actually putting the price increase at 70 per cent. Environment Minister Michael Howard announced to a roaring House of Commons that the companies would be summonsed to explain why a rise of more than 10 per cent was needed. He said there was nothing in the government's proposals for privatising the water industry that justified such enormous increases.

The water companies had decided to disclose the size of their charges following a government announcement that the ten Water Authorities would be increasing their charges by up to 13 per cent. What followed then was a mess. In an interview on Channel 4 on 6 February, Secretary of State Nicholas Ridley admitted that the government had no powers whatsoever to curb the planned price rises. This was followed by another leak emanating from Ernst Whinney which more or less accused the government of reneging on a private agreement to see company charges increased to match those of the Water Authorities. It disclosed that Mr Howard himself had since pressed the phasing in of new charges, although refusing to accept that they should be raised over a short period. In effect this meant the government had gone back on its understanding with the water companies, 'an understanding which the WCA's Director and advisers considered to have been reached with the DoE on 1 December'. In the event, Michael Howard failed in his attempt to stop the private water companies raising their tariffs.

On 7 February newspapers were running headlines such as, 'Ministers "Confused" Over Result of Water Sell Off'. It was at this stage that the government announced that it intended to impose a guillotine on the Water Bill, thus limiting its further discussion. The MPs taking part in the Committee stage had spent seventy-five hours debating the first nine clauses of the 180 clause bill. The guillotine motion – which was passed, of course – limited that Committee to a further seventy-eight hours to debate the remaining 181 clauses. Twenty-three and a half hours were allowed for its Report stage and Third Reading.

Government Chief Whip John Wakeham had told the House that if the government was to arrange for the sale of shares towards the end of 1989, then consideration of the bill had to be speeded up. This particular session ended in great acrimony with government spokesmen referring to Labour's record on the water industry in the 1970s and Shadow Leader of the House Frank Dobson describing the government's appointee as chairman of the NRA, Lord Crickhowell, as 'old and stupid' . . . 'If the NRA is to command the respect of everyone in this country, it should not be headed by a partisan appointee getting £40,000 a year for three days a week.'

Nothing was made any clearer some weeks later when, speaking on the Radio 4 programme *The World This Weekend*, Nicholas Ridley actually said that privatising water would bring prices down! He said there were two different issues at stake.

One is privatisation, which will make them more efficient and actually bring the price of water down a little bit because it will be more efficiently done. Secondly, there is the very large amount of money that has to be invested in improving our treatment works, our pipes, our sewage works and many other aspects of the water industry as well. This will cost a lot of money, though the two are not, of course, the same thing. And privatisation will reduce the otherwise large increase that will take place due to environmental improvements which everybody, I think, would like to see take place.

Hovering over everything is the question of the EEC Directives. Michael Howard acknowledged that it would take Britain six years to comply with the most important European standards for drinking water but has maintained that this will not interfere with the privatisation timetable.

Since Mrs Thatcher came to power in 1979 she has received the plaudits of an almost entirely adulatory press. We would need to go back to the mediaeval monarchs to match the buckets-full of praise which have been heaped on her unstintingly by the media, skilfully managed by her Press Office and her chief Press Officer, Mr Bernard Ingham. No other Prime Minister, not even the man she familiarly refers to as 'Winston', has had such an easy ride. It therefore came as more of a shock when a good deal of overtly adverse comment began to appear in the newspapers, some of it in those which do not usually criticise her, for by the spring it was apparent that the scheme was in disarray. Rattled by the announcement of the price hike by the private water companies, she told the Commons on 7 February 1989, first, that the increases were based on past rises that were much lower than those of the ten Water Authorities, then she said the rises 'had no point at all' since all charges would be subject to control after the November sale.

A selection of headlines makes the point: 'Tories Losing Fight in Water Sell Off', 'Risk of Drowning in Water Sell Off', 'Ridley "Must Win" in Water Battle', 'The Wrong Way to Sell Water', 'Pollution Report Suppressed and Rewritten' and 'Wet and Worrying'. Various commentators noted that the government appeared to be surprised at the decision of the private water companies to hoist their prices and wondered why this should be so. If, as it now appears, we are finally being dragged into line with the EEC, then a great deal needs to be spent to bring our water up to standard and as the excuse of cutbacks on public spending cannot be used, there is no alternative but to raise prices once water is administered entirely by private companies. Nor can customers use the free market to buy cheaper water for there will not be, there cannot possibly be, any competition. A public monopoly will merely become a private monopoly.

One of the Prime Minister's least favourite newspapers, *The Observer*, put it well when it said that

> even its firmest supporters must recognise that in its rush to privatise water the Government has gone in over its head and is now slowly sinking in an ideological bog of its own making. The guillotine motion may speed the passage of the legislation through Parliament, but it does nothing to answer the serious doubts being voiced in the City, the water industry, and not least on the Tory backbenches, about the wisdom of seeking to sell off the most natural of all natural monopolies.

These doubts unfortunately coincided with a crass and patronising advertising campaign which even the government was finally forced to admit had failed abysmally. It showed 'watermen' delivering milk like milkmen, stacking up thousands of crates outside homes.

Speaking at a Conservative local government conference on 5 March, the Prime Minister appeared to go some way towards admitting that the plan to privatise water had become a public relations disaster, in spite of all the marketing. She told them, to their surprise, 'I know that the subject of privatisation of water has not in fact been handled well or accurately.' This was interpreted in many quarters as criticism of the two hapless ministers in charge – Nicholas Ridley and Michael Howard – but the public relations machine was almost immediately wheeled out to correct this misunderstanding. The Prime Minister had in fact meant the disobedient media which, on this issue, had not fallen into line. Challenged later to say if she had intended to criticise her Secretary of State for the Environment, she responded: 'No, he is the best environment secretary we have ever had.' Mr Ridley himself said that her remark was an attack on the media and critics in the Labour Party. 'I entirely agree that the mishandling by the Labour Party and the Press on this whole issue has been very sad. She is quite right that the essential importance of this measure has been misunderstood.'

One of Mrs Thatcher's strangest comments during the conference was when she said, rejecting the idea that water was much too essential a commodity to risk putting it into private hands, 'food is important. But you don't go to a national food cooperative shop where you only have one choice.' Neither do you go to one private food shop to buy all your food.

The problem now is that the Prime Minister has staked her personal reputation on privatising water and when that happens nothing must get in the way of it. It happened with the National Health Service when, under pressure over manifest discontent and rising public concern over its lack of funding, she suddenly announced during a *Panorama* interview that there was going to be a substantial Health Review. One wonders if it was entirely off the top of her head. It seemed to take everyone by surprise and the subsequent hurried documents, based on information supplied entirely by people who do not work in the NHS, are bringing their own tranche of problems. She is an activist who likes to take a hand in everything and we are continually told that she is 'incandescent' or 'furious' when things do not go her way, and that she is about to take charge of everything from street litter to football hooliganism.

Without giving any consideration to the problems of rate capped local authorities, many of which have been forced to put street cleaning out to inefficient private operators, a photocall was organised showing Mrs Thatcher picking up some previously strewn litter in St James's Park. Her desire to be seen active over football hooliganism has led to a complicated scheme that not even the police like, and which does not in any way address the larger problem of gangs of hooligans who follow football matches, fighting it out in the streets outside the grounds. So, now, with water. She is to take personal charge of the campaign.

It was summed up well in a leader in *The Independent* (6 March 1989), headlined 'The Perils of an Activist PM'. Mrs Thatcher has at last, it says, noticed that water privatisation is unpopular. 'She does not, however, wish to admit that there is anything mistaken about the idea, or about the energy with which she has pushed for its implementation.' She has therefore decided it is the *way* in which it is being handled which is objectionable, not the thing itself. Her ambiguous remarks on the way privatisation has been handled seemed to leave her scope to dispense with Nicholas Ridley as she has with other ministers who have faithfully carried out her wishes in the past, so that if the going got tough she could distance herself from him and he could join the long, long queue of other ex-ministers who have embarrassed her. (In fact, since writing the foregoing, she has done just that and replaced him with the younger, and more acceptable Chris Patten.) Her message is that it is the presentation that is wrong and to that end, at the time of writing, Michael Howard is stomping the country trying to get the real benefits of privatisation across.

The inept water ads have been paid for by the Water Authorities (that is, largely by us) at a cost of £21.8m. These were designed, say the authorities, merely to raise 'awareness' and were not connected with privatisation proper. Documents leaked to the BBC, however (*Panorama*, 4 September 1989), show that these and the privatisation adverts to come were all part of the same programme. A survey of those who had bought shares in other privatised industries and who watched these adverts showed that 62 per cent would not buy shares in water. During the height of the first part of the campaign the Water Authorities were spending more than the budgets for Nescafé Gold Blend, Persil, Coca-Cola and Guinness put together. It will cost a further £18m at least for the privatisation adverts proper. This raises the whole principle of the amount of public money being spent on selling off national assets; an issue which is likely to become a hot political potato. Where do you draw the increasingly thin grey line between information and party propaganda. The money spent by the government on advertising – our money, taxpayers' money, which we are always being told must be spent with such great care that it cannot be used on sewers, or nurses' wages, or more school books – has risen nearly fivefold in four years according to Treasury figures (*Financial Times*, 27 March 1989). In May, the Treasury estimated that the budget for the financial year just ended would top a staggering £97m, with another £70m spent on promotions, publicity and leaflets. It was then estimated that the budget for 1989–90 would be even more enormous with £20m spent on advertising water alone, and a similar sum on selling off electricity. By the end of the summer these figures had to be updated again. The government's advertising budget has risen from £35m in 1979–80 to £150m in 1988–9. Unless action is taken it will go on rising.

The two months before the run-up to privatisation will see us deluged with media publicity assuring us that it is a great idea from which we will all benefit. Will it work? Not on present showing. Ordinary people just do not like the idea and in March there were two small straws in the wind. Twenty-five thousand people in the Truro area of Cornwall signed a petition against it which their MP, Matthew Taylor, delivered to Downing Street. On a west coast beach, other protestors floated off an effigy of the Prime Minister, seated on a lavatory, into a sea heavily polluted with the raw sewage she had told television viewers was always treated before being released.

To return to that leader in *The Independent*.

> A Government led by a less determined Prime Minister would have decided that the game was not worth the candle. Mrs Thatcher lacks the temperament to accept that line of thought. She is an activist. She must always be reforming something. Her vast energies, which have on occasion served her party so well, now seem to threaten its electoral popularity; not a danger which the relevant minister, Mr Ridley, can be depended on to understand.

Only time will tell if this surmise is correct. The government has survived a host of challenges, which would have brought down almost any of its predecessors, with its electoral popularity almost intact. Our fragmented opposition and our electoral system have combined to ensure that its parliamentary majority will enable it to put through any piece of legislation it chooses. It will be interesting to see if water privatisation finally proves to be its Achilles' heel.

13

The French Connection

The increasing financial involvement of French water companies has already been touched on but it is perhaps worth considering in rather more detail just what this means. Again, I am indebted to NALGO which has made a particular study of the subject and which undertook research in France with the help of the CGT – Confédération Générale du Travail – the equivalent of our TUC.

Once it became known that the British government was to sell off water, a good many predators immediately became interested. An obvious way in was to buy into the existing statutory private companies which is what happened. It is worth repeating, says NALGO in its report on the French Water industry, 'that these companies offered the *only* means for private capital to be invested in the water industry'. The most interesting development has been the extent to which three French companies have bought in – Compagnie Générale des Eaux, Lyonnaise des Eaux and SAUR. Together these three companies supply water to 65 per cent of French consumers on behalf of the municipalities. These municipalities remain responsible for the supply of water and the treatment of sewage but in many cases they contract this out to the three companies.

In a letter to *The Guardian* (10 March 1989), Alan Jackson of the Water Section of NALGO explained exactly how this works out in practice. Mrs Thatcher, he says, was wrong in saying that

French water is in private hands because it offers the consumer a better service.

Firstly the French water industry is approximately split between 60% in the private sector and 40% in the public sector.

Secondly, the 60% in the private sector is franchised. French towns, cities and municipalities put their water and sewerage services out to tender but retain control of the franchise which may last for anything between 20 and 30 years. When the franchise runs out it can either be renewed or offered to another operator, public or private, if the service has not proved satisfactory. The main point here is that the town, city or municipality retains ultimate control of the franchise, e.g. *public control*. The proposed water privatisation in this country is on the basis of handing water and sewerage services lock stock and barrel over to the private sector – with no public control or accountability. there is nowhere in the world where a wholly private water supply and sewage disposal system exists.

Under a franchise the contractor operates and maintains the plant owned by the municipality. There is also a *concession* system where the municipality hands over entire responsibility to a contractor who owns the plant, materials and labour although such concessions are rare. Two smaller systems are that of *gerance* – where a contractor simply collects the charges on a cost plus fee basis (a sophisticated billing system) – or *service* where such things as meter readings are put out.

There is no national fixed fee for water charges – these are fixed by the municipalities. It cannot be stressed strongly enough that all these negotiations are undertaken by *elected* representatives. River pollution comes under the province of six River Basin Authorities, funded by a 2 per cent levy on water charges with grants awarded to municipalities who undertake improvement schemes.

So to the three French companies who are so interested in what will be our totally free market in water.

Lyonnaise des Eaux

Its consolidated revenues in 1987 were £1.75bn. Worldwide it employs 33,089 people plus a further *8 million* through affiliates in the USA, Europe and Asia. Its French workforce is 4,298 distributed around fourteen regional areas serving a population of 10 million. It is also France's principal *funeral* director, conducting over 40 per cent of French funerals. It owns thirteen cable TV networks and a part share in Club Mediterranean.

The company told the NALGO delegation in October 1988 that it sought worldwide expansion and is interested in Britain. At first, it could not see a way in but then, with the prospect of water privatisation, it became very interested indeed. It has, therefore, built up the controlling stake in Essex (98.2 per cent) and East Anglia (a 89 per cent holding). It also has a small stake in the Bristol Waterworks Company. It intends taking seats on the various boards and already has two on Essex SWC. The company made it quite clear that it intends calling on its considerable scientific and engineering resources back in France. The company drew the attention of NALGO to a French law which obliges all companies to sell 3 per cent of their equity to their employees – this will not, of course, be the case here.

The company has well-established industrial relations with its trade unions with negotiations carried out by the company's headquarters on behalf of relevant subsidiaries. Employees in the water industry automatically have their basic salaries increased in line with the civil service, and their electrical divisions follow the pattern set by the French electricity supply industry. Within the company they have regular monthly meetings with national union officials.

Lyonnaise has already established a joint company with Laings called Water Services Ltd. This could obviously be used for further expansion into the British water industry.

Compagnie Générale des Eaux

This is the largest of the three water companies, with total consolidated sales for 1987 of £5.56bn. Water supply accounts for 23.6 per cent of the group's income. Its other activities include public works building construction, home building, property development, communications and leisure. It supplies water to 20 million people in 7,500 communities. The company told NALGO it would seek to place people on the SWC Boards and exercise its influence from the top down. Interestingly, it does feel it can cash in as people in Britain begin to demand higher water standards (especially regarding nitrates) than currently obtain here. It foresees greater contact and exchanges between French and English staff. It expects to buy a significant share in the PLCs on flotation and become a real presence in the British water industry. Under French law employees have to be invited to board meetings. That will not obtain here.

Employees of CGE have their salaries based on local government scales although each subsidiary company has its own arrangements. The company meets frequently with representatives of the five recognised trade unions on an informal basis. For more specific purposes, formal meetings are arranged. In Marseilles and Lille, it has set up joint companies with Lyonnaise and insists this was because those municipalities had wanted this to ensure greater security of service. It was stressed that in Britain it would *not* be working as a contractor for local government but as a totally independent private company.

It buys in its supplies from various contractors but owns a company manufacturing water meters. CGE expressed a wish to develop and produce its own chemical treatments. It expects to obtain its requirements from the cheapest source and if this is French, then so be it. It is proud of its 'denitrification plant' and expressed surprise at how slow the British water industry has been to deal with the problem. Their main concern over buying into British water is how much of the capital debt the government will write off and who will pay to clean up supplies and modernise waste disposal.

SAUR (Société d'Aménagement
Urbain et Rural)

SAUR is part of the massive French Bouygues group, a huge multinational with a revenue for 1987 of £5.6bn. SAUR contributed £336m to this. The group's interests include construction, engineering, property development, home building, municipal services, television, electricity distribution and specialist waterproofing services. SAUR supplies water to 1.5 million people and 11 million worldwide. Bouygues has extensive interests in Africa, especially on the Ivory Coast.

SAUR was immediately interested in the coming flotation and initially set up a joint venture with Trafalgar House – Cementation SAUR – but the partnership ended as it was not found to be satisfactory. SAUR UK is now an independent company headed by a Mr John Standsby. SAUR wants to be in as strong a position as possible to take advantage of the privatisation of water and has made no secret of this. It intends using its British subsidiary as a holding company to take stakes in the SWCs but sees itself in partnership with British workers, not replacing them with French staff. In fact, the company told NALGO, that it now sees its plans for the UK as stretching far beyond water and into the whole public service sector. In France, negotiations with workers are in the context of the whole Bouygues group and company unionism is preferred. Staff relations are apparently very paternalistic with a high standard of staff services. In the company's headquarters there are shops, banks, hairdressers, cinemas, travel agents, theatres and a gymnasium, all for the use of staff and guests. The site is virtually 'cashless', a plastic company card giving access to any facility.

SAUR, it seems, is adopting a very competitive stance with regard to investing in the UK and will take every opportunity that comes up. Referring to its failed partnership with Trafalgar House, the company told NALGO that SAUR UK Ltd under Mr John Standsby, was now involved in our offshore oil exploration industry. It would also like to find new private sector partners with whom to do business.

After researching the subject in France, NALGO felt that

it was a matter of very real concern that the French-based multinationals which are involved in water are intent on spreading into as many UK interests as possible, especially after the free-for-all in 1992. According to consumers and unions, the record of the French-based companies in France 'as providers of an essential service, in maintaining the environment and as employers, is far from satisfactory'. After privatisation the government will, in effect, be passing ownership of our water industry over to, among others, these French multinationals. Waiting on the sidelines too for the rich pickings involved are companies in the USA, Japan, Australia and the Far East. But the French companies have a head start both in water and through that as a bridge to a whole range of other services from electricity to telecommunications. 'Their experience in these fields is greater than many UK companies currently trying to operate in these areas. The French multinationals are poised to wipe the board.' Put simply – if water privatisation goes ahead, this country will lose control of its own water industry.

14

The Rip Off –
Or That's Where
You Come In

Currently, when you pay your water charges you pay for the cost of receiving the water you use, its treatment before reaching you and the disposal of your sewage. You have the right of access to hundreds of thousands of acres of land around rivers and reservoirs, some of it amongst the most beautiful there is in the British Isles. You would, even if the government had properly invested in cleaning up our water and repairing the infrastructure, have had to pay more for your water but you are also immune from paying out for a whole range of totally unnecessary expenses – but not for long.

You are now about to pay for the whole thing: the cost of the flotation of the private companies, which will run into millions of pounds; advertising them widely in the written media and on TV, which will cost more millions; paying for the hugely enhanced salaries of the water board chairmen (there are no women) once they chair private companies; for the profit all the shareholders will expect – and all before we use a single drop of water! It is a 'scam' on such a scale it takes the breath away. It is almost funny. And on top of all that you won't be able to take your custom elsewhere if you think your new PLC is fleecing you for the service it gives you – unless you move house.

When you have finished paying for all that, think of the billions it is going to cost to bring our water up to EEC standards.

You will also lose all you and preceding generations have already put into the Water Authorities, through the money paid out for capital plant and improved services by the local authorities. In fact some local authorities are currently planning court action to see what they can do about the sale of 'their' assets.

It is hardly surprising that the government is being pretty coy about what the flotation will cost, but we can have some idea from the fact that it cost around £20m to sell off British Gas. When it comes to the flotation of water there is a very real problem. Company shareholders, whether of existing companies, new ones, those which have merged or taken each other over, expect their company to grow ever bigger and more profitable. But it is very difficult to see how this can happen with a water PLC because the amount of water consumed in the UK is relatively stable – people are not going to be persuaded to use twice as much by an advertising campaign, however subtle. Nor can they be seduced into using one water company's product rather than that of another because they will have no choice. There is no growth potential in cleaning up rivers and if there is a profit to be made on the development of Water Authority land, then that will be a one-off bonanza.

So the government will probably float off the companies as 'safe income stocks', but this will cause the aforementioned problems since the return might well not be high enough to attract prospective investors. Even if the Water Authorities can be dressed up as an excellent investment, then the separate authorities which will form the new PLCs will differ widely as to just how attractive they might be in the long term. Thames Water is the wealthiest and therefore has the biggest potential attraction but who will want North West Water with its collapsing nineteenth-century sewers? Or South West Water with the possible long-term consequences of the Lowermoor incident?

The biggest give away, of course, will be those Water Authority assets, estimated at about £27bn pounds – currently owned by *all of us*. They will, no doubt, act as a considerable sweetener.

The Treasury has set a target of £6bn for the flotation. As

JAWS points out in *Water Down the Drain?* this means that the water PLCs will have to raise £720m a year to pay the dividends (assuming a 12 per cent dividend rate, which is about average). This amounts to 'a third of then current authorities *total* (my italics) income'. However, if it is decided to write off the industry's existing capital, debts would reduce the proceeds of the sale of the century to a mere £1bn.

Additional revenue can, therefore, only be raised by increasing costs and by actually cutting back on capital investment rather than in increasing it. Revenue will also have to be raised to pay Corporation Tax as Water Authorities are currently exempt from it – they have been able to finance expenditure on assets without incurring taxation for so doing. After privatisation water companies will be just like any other commercial companies making anything from chemicals to socks, cars to property development.

Just what the fate of the private statutory water companies will be after privatisation remains somewhat unclear. If the constitutional links between them and the Water Authorities are broken, then the companies could be brought into line with the new WSPLCs but it is difficult to see what the future will hold for them as they only distribute water. The most likely outcome will be that they will eventually be taken over and swallowed up by the new WSPLCs – who in turn can take over each other or be taken over by other companies entirely.

How will you be billed in future? Well, the obvious way is by metering as is the case with electricity and gas. In April 1988, national water metering trials were instigated and the result appears to show that the quantity of water used immediately reduces when this happens. During the debate on the Second Reading of the Water Bill John Cunningham gave an example of how one of these trials is working out. He read from a letter he had received from a resident of Brookmans Park in Hertfordshire.

I am part of the water meter trials in the Lee Valley area. From next April my water will be metered on a two part tariff basis. Peak rates will occur at 7 am–10 am and 6 pm–9 pm, exactly the time when one uses water for personal hygiene. Lee Valley have admitted to me . . . that because people use less water when metered, they have already raised the charges between ten and fifteen per cent. They also admit that if people are very frugal with their water consumption, prices will be increased further to maintain an 'adequate' revenue.

By next April I will be paying between 15–20 per cent more for my water and the overall water bill will probably increase by 25 per cent. All this before privatisation. What will the charges be after? Frankly, I can only say that it will be a 'huge rip off'.

And that is just what you are likely to pay for the water. You will also pay for the cost of the meters as well. It is estimated that the cost of installing them will be around £2,000m, money that could instead be invested in improving facilities and levels of service. Householders will have to pay about £100 just for the privilege of having the meter installed, with no promise of any better service in return.

What happens if you just can't pay? Too bad. In spite of the tub thumping about our booming economy, we have an enormous underclass of the poor and very poor with more families living below the poverty line now than for a very long time. For the very poor, struggling with possible loss of housing benefit, unemployment, loans instead of grants for necessities and spiralling electricity costs (to pay for *that* privatisation), water will be just another blow. Large, poor families will economise on water to meet their other bills which will certainly take us swiftly back to Victorian values in terms of disease. It will pose a very real threat to public health.

Speaking during the Committee stage on the Water Bill, David Hinchcliffe MP asked how the better-off members of that Committee might manage their budgets if, like some of his constituents, their wages (not benefits) were only £82 a week from which £10 a week might be deducted to pay a previous water debt while £40 already went on rent. 'I accept that he would also receive DSS support and child benefit, but how would he manage to support a family on that money?' As a social worker in Leeds before entering Parliament, he had found all too many people who had had their gas or electricity cut off, not because they did not want to pay it but because their income quite simply was insufficient for them to meet all their essential bills. 'That is not mismanagement; they were poor.'

What happens to those who are already on the poverty line exercised the minds of a number of MPs during the Committee stage of the bill, and they came away unsatisfied with the replies they received. A proportion of MPs felt that water was not in the same category as gas or electricity, that because of its public health implications cutting off the supply should never be an option. As Allan Roberts said, cutting off gas and electricity can be very brutal – leading to the deaths of elderly people from hypothermia during a bad winter – 'but it would rarely have public health implications for the neighbours and the community'. Cutting off water, thus promoting disease, would.

Comprehensive figures on water disconnections at present were, he said, hard to come by which was in itself worrying. According to the Under Secretary of State for the Environment (19 July 1988), information on disconnections is not collected by that department. From the figures Mr Roberts had been able to find, they showed a rise from 2,052 in 1984–5 to 7,120 in 1987–8. When the Welsh figures are added to those previously given (which were for England alone), the total reaches 9,187, a jump of 24 per cent on the previous year. In the previous two years, the figure jumped 63 and 112 per cent respectively. One reason for the rise, he notes, is that before April 1988 the benefit system included sensible arrangements for budgeting for and paying water charges. After April 1988 this sensible arrangement was discontinued.

Statistics show that the bulk of households that have their water supply disconnected are families with children, continued Mr Roberts. There is also concern for households with one or more disabled members. Both these groups have high water consumption and inadequate incomes. How will costs be recouped by the companies? 'The public are not stupid. If we all have meters installed and we all economise so that the bills are not high, the basic cost of water provision will have to be recovered and we shall be hit by a standing charge. The elderly and the large families who try and economise will be hit both ways.'

He went on to give examples such as the disabled couple in Merthyr Tydfil who had to carry all their water in buckets as they had been cut off because they could not pay their water charges out of their invalidity benefit, and the man in Mildenhall who was unable to pay off his water debt for eighteen months and so had to bury his own excrement in the garden.

> If my next door neighbour was cut off there would be a considerable health risk to me. It would be in my self-interest, as well as being the act of a Good Samaritan, to help that neighbour by providing water for the necessary functions of maintaining a clean, hygienic house that does not constitute a health risk. What happens to a person who helps in that way? Is he treated in the same way as a person who supplies electricity or gas to someone who is cut off? Is it a criminal offence? Can one ask a neighbour for a cup of sugar or a glass of milk but not for a glass of water because one might be committing an offence?

He was supported in his view by Chris Mullin who told how a couple of pensioners came to his surgery about the loss of around £8 off their housing benefits. 'They had led hard lives and that showed in their faces. They were in their early 70s and not in good health. We wrote down the facts of their case and as they shuffled towards the door, she said to him, "I suppose there will be the poll tax next." He replied, "Don't worry, love, with any luck we'll be gone by then."' In fact, he said, the Poll Tax would not be next – first would come the water charges, then electricity privatisation, then more benefit charges and only after that, the Poll Tax.

It is not melodramatic to consider what will happen if a lot of people find they have to ration their water or find themselves without a supply. From the aesthetic point of view smelly people in dirty clothes are not pleasant to have around and there will be far more of them. Baths and changes of clothing will be the first things to go, but lack of cleanliness breeds illness and lack of a tolerable water supply breeds epidemics.

Come back Joseph Chamberlain. One hundred years on we are prepared to go back to the very kind of conditions you sought to remedy!

To recap briefly, after privatisation the cost of your water will include:

- Repairs to the neglected infrastructure owing to lack of investment over the years;
- Cleaning up the water to meet the higher standards of the EEC;
- Installing water meters;
- Paying the cost of meter readers, administrators, the clerical work involved, etc.;
- The cost of advertising the sale – which will be in millions;
- Flotation costs – likewise;
- Shareholders' profits;
- Corporation Tax;
- Higher executive salaries;
- Goodies for those executives. This was well put by Mr Roy Watts of Thames Water, quoted in Hansard (7 December 1989). He said: 'I see a lot of fun – playing hard, working hard. I see a sports ground, I see a training centre – I even see an executive helicopter.'

You, of course, will be paying for that expensive toy and his hike in salary – similar executives in the other privatised industries received salary increases of up to 160 per cent.

And all this just so that you can get clean drinking water out of your tap . . .

15

Private – Keep Out!

Estimates vary slightly as to just how much land is currently 'ours' and is administered by the Water Authorities, but it is at least 455,765 acres and the Countryside Commission estimates that some 335,000 acres are of conservation or recreational interest.

Some of the most beautiful of our English landscapes are owned by the Water Authorities and have remained that way because of their very special position. They include 39,000 acres of the Lake District National Park, 12,000 acres of the Brecon Beacons, 5,000 acres of Snowdonia and 850 acres of Exmoor. Even Haworth Moor, made famous in Emily Brontë's *Wuthering Heights*, is owned by North West Water. The Peak District could lose free public access to twenty-three square miles of moorland and a further forty miles of footpath through some of its finest countryside.

There seems little end to what this land – and resources such as reservoirs – can be used for after privatisation. Obviously, development of all kinds will be a major factor, restricted use of reservoirs another, and what will happen to the open access to the countryside currently owned by the authorities for those who just want to ramble, hike or picnic in it? There are no safeguards in the bill and in fact amendments trying to ensure open free access were defeated.

In *Liquid Assets*, a report prepared in 1988 by researchers at Leeds University for the Council for the Preservation of Rural

England, there are some examples of what has already happened. The first concerns Thames Water.

Thames Water's assets are currently estimated at around £1bn and the authority has already adopted a radical commercial approach to their development. Between 1987 and 1988 it increased the sale of land it considered 'surplus' by 94 per cent which brought it in £9m. It has embarked on a joint venture with Wimpey in the development of thirty-eight acres at the Queen Elizabeth Reservoir, Walton-on-Thames, building 458 highly priced homes.

The development of the London ring main has rendered five of its reservoir sites redundant for water services operations and the authority is now developing the sites to raise an estimated 25 to 30 per cent of the cost of providing the new ring main. The sites involved are at Stoke Newington, Kempton East and West, Barn Elms, Surbiton and Hornsey. The environments, says the CPRE, vary from greenfield sites such as Kempton (which are sites of Special Scientific Interest) to urban green sites of significant conservation and public amenity value in deprived inner city areas like Stoke Newington. Plans for Stoke Newington are well advanced. The ninety-three-acre site includes two reservoirs and filter beds, identified as being of conservation value in a report commissioned by the London Wildlife Trust in 1985, and is a major amenity to a very deprived community. It is considered of national importance for two species of wildfowl and remains part of a system of waters with nationally important wildfowl populations.

The Thames Water development will involve building over 80 per cent of the site including extensive luxury housing on the East reservoir (the one with the highest conservation value) in order, according to the *Evening Standard* (24 February 1988), to take advantage of the area's rising property market. The plan also includes combining nature conservation and recreational interests on the West reservoir, together with 200,000 square feet of commercial shopping, office and warehousing on the filter beds. About 80 per cent of the site would disappear altogether under brick. The local residents have opposed the scheme.

Says the CPRE:

In response to the controversy surrounding its proposals for the Stoke Newington scheme, TWA has put forward a scheme for financing conservation and amenity protection (i.e. non-profitable aspects of current water authorities statutory duties) through a Trust Fund representing 2% of the profits generated from the development process. This represents a worrying model for the future as it builds into the system the sacrifice of many acres and sites of environmental value as the price for preserving the few.

TWA's activities illustrate the direct link between development profits and financing capital investment under a privatised industry and some of the range of potential development strategies. Moreover, through their proposal to create 'environmental trusts' using a small percentage of profits from development to finance environmental work, they illustrate one of the possible routes which threaten to draw conservationists into the development process itself.

The CPRE then turns its attention to another development aspect – water-based recreation. It lists the kinds of activities currently enjoyed: game fishing, coarse fishing, sailing, sailboarding, canoeing, rowing, subaqua, water skiing and, around the reservoirs, horse riding and bird watching. Amenities provided include picnic sites, country parks, fishing lodges, information centres, viewing points, car parks, toilets, nature reserves, nature trails, footpaths, disabled amenities and educational facilities. Many such sites are of Special Scientific Interest. The new WSPLCs will be under fierce pressure to develop these sites for profit.

Rutland Water is a site of Special Scientific Interest for its internationally important population of wintering wildfowl. It is a candidate for listing as a Special Protection Area under EEC Directive 79/409 on the Conservation of Wild Birds and also as a special 'wetlands' site. It has a nature reserve managed by the Leicestershire and Rutland Conservation Trust, which is unfortunately depending on the Water Authority which grants it its licence and meets the management costs and the warden's salary. It has recently become an area of conflict between conservationists and its owner, Anglian Water, who have pursued an increasingly commercial policy towards recreational activity on the reservoir, culminating, says the CPRE, 'in the contravention of Section 28 of the Wildlife and Countryside Act of 1985 when it failed to consult with the Nature Conservancy Council over its proposals to extend fishing rights on the reservoir. More recently the surrounding farmland has been subject to speculative buying and selling with private developers looking to gain permission for extensive leisure developments using the reservoir as a major attraction.'

The report continues:

There is growing encroachment of new recreational facilities and commercial interests on the reservoir. Currently three main recreational developments are taking place. The first of these is the intensification and privatisation of fishing. The fishing rights were privatised in 1987 when Anglian Water sold them on a nine-year lease to a private management company. Before the sale, Anglian Water extended the permissible fishing period in the winter months, which are the most disruptive to wildlife, without seeking NCC consent. When the NCC challenged the decision, Anglian Water threatened the NCC with legal action on commercial grounds for seeking to 'undermine the viability of the fishing and the sale of rights'.

Next comes the intensification and privatisation of sailing and related activities. Sailing is provided in two areas – a 'public' concession leased out by Anglian Water to a private individual and managed on a pay-by-the-day basis, mainly for local users (who hire boats including windsurfers) in the South East, and a private club with a long lease of thirty to forty years negotiated in 1974–5 for those willing to pay high fees only. In addition, Anglian Water have now licensed a pleasure cruiser run by a private concern. Sailing and sail-boarding has increased particularly in the autumn and winter months, which again causes concern to conservationists because of its effect on migratory wildfowl.

On top of all that a development company has been active and turned a country house bordering on the shores of the reservoir into a country club/hotel with time share chalets in the grounds. It has also attempted to develop the site further, seeking planning permission for more time share chalets but planning permission was refused. It also wants to build a ninety bed hotel attached to an eighteen-hole golf complex at Lyndon on the western edge of the reservoir. At the time the CPRE report was prepared outline planning permission had been granted for the golf complex. A second property company attempted to gain permission for another eighteen-hole golf course and another hotel at the northern end of the reservoir, at Eagleton, but did not succeed in getting planning permission so sold the holding on to another developer.

In the Peak District, a long-standing relationship between conservationists and the Water Authorities appears to have come to an abrupt end. Roland Smith, head of information at the Peak Park Joint Planning Board told *The Guardian* (26 January 1989) how useful that partnership had proved in the past but

> the attitude of the water authorities has changed. In the past we've done some very constructive things with them. We've won awards for partnership schemes. Now all that is suddenly threatened. We've found our allies measuring up car parks, which have always been free and jointly provided, for pay booths. We've found fences going up across open moorland with no consultation at all. They're parcelling up everything into little plots ready to sell off. It's just happening – they've been charged to do it. Years of co-operation on conservation and recreation are going down the drain.

Three different Water Authorities own land in the Peak Park – Severn Trent, Yorkshire and North West (about 15 per cent of the total area). The park authority, according to Mr Smith, tried to get assurances from the three of them that all would be well after privatisation, but to no avail. North West Water actually sought planning applications against the park's policy on large-scale tourist developments, including one for a big water sports centre at the Bottoms Reservoir in Longdendale. The park authority encourages only environmentally sensitive development and, as a planning authority, said no to the scheme. At the time of writing it is going to appeal. This is unprecedented in the history of national parks.

North West Water has also threatened to terminate access agreements, their letter stating that the authority was obviously in a position to remove the concessionary rights and might do so at any time. At present ramblers and walkers have free access to large areas of the Peak and they do not even have to keep to footpaths. In return the park authority pays a nominal rent which is up for review in 1991 and, says Mr Smith, 'we are worried about what price we're going to be talking about'.

There are also woodlands and the shores of the reservoirs which are available to the public and about twenty car parks with public toilets and information services under joint management. The joint management of Water Authorities and Peak Park Authority also runs woodland conservation schemes, field wall restoration and heather regeneration. A partnership scheme with Severn Trent which has operated for the last five years at the Ladybower dam in upper Derwent valley won a major conservation award last year.

The area gets a million visitors a year and the park authority provides a traffic management scheme which closes off the road at busy times, lays on mini buses for people to use, cycle hire, car parks and picnic areas, along with Rangers, for which the cost is shared 50/50 between the park and the Water Authorities. 'Who will pay the other half after privatisation?' asks Mr Smith.

At present, the Water Authorities have statutory responsibility for recreation and conservation under the 1973 Water Act. The Peak Park Authority wants similar provision after privatisation and has put forward constructive ideas for safeguards to be built into the Act, such as a code of practice on conservation and recreation for the new bodies when they come into being, together with further conservation safeguards on the land before they sell it off. But it does not appear that any heed will be taken of what the park authority has to propose, for there is little point in Water Authorities being tied down in such a way if the aim of government is for them to sell off their assets to the highest bidder.

Being a National Park will not save the Peak District, not any more, not now that anything and everything is for sale. In the middle of Langdale, in the Lake District, there is now a time share leisure complex, complete with 'Caribbean' swimming pool and at Llangattock, in the Brecon Beacons, a developer is trying to get planning permission for a series of mock mediaeval villages containing 240 half-timbered holiday cottages with central, glass-covered leisure facilities inside which would be a gym, exotic landscaping and artificial waterfalls. In the Pembrokeshire Coast National Park, a developer wants to build 160 chalets on the cliff top near Amroth, while another is planning a thirty-two-acre time share complex near Tenby. The most the government has been prepared to do with relation to the Water Authorities is to put in a clause saying that they will have to consult the parks over any changes to existing agreements and public access. Similar 'consultation' agreements exist for health authorities who want to close down hospital wards and whole hospitals and it is apparent just how successful this has been.

The outlook is a bleak one. According to Environment Minister Michael Howard, he who is in charge of water privatisation, land policy on property not directly used for water operations will depend on the 'goodwill and commonsense' of water operators' subsidiary companies – that is, the private companies set up by water suppliers to manage their land after privatisation. In fact they will be free to disregard special legislative safeguards on conservation and public access. Although, as a sop to public anxiety, a highly detailed code of practice was issued by the government at the end of January 1989, this will apply only to land directly related to water supply and waterworks. Mr Howard conceded, therefore, that huge areas of land 'may not be covered by the code'.

The admission came following a letter from the Department of the Environment to Thames Water of which Dr John Cunningham received a copy. The letter stated that the proposed statutory duties would only apply to the PLC 'core' business since it 'would be impossible to justify a blanket extension to subsidiary companies'. These subsidiaries, said the letter, 'would be no different from other private companies wholly unconnected with the PLC'. Dr Cunningham stated that this proved there was a big hole in the legislation and that the code of practice was useless in the face of it.

It is in the interests of the Water Authorities that there are as few strings as possible attached to privatisation, since any kind of restriction could seriously detract from the investment attractions at flotation. While the government has told the authorities that when they become PLCs profits from the sale of assets should be ploughed back into the business, a number of them are working on ways of saving some of the profits from the ensuing property bonanza for their shareholders, according to *The Independent* (21 February 1989). This is one reason for the setting up of the private companies to manage the land assets, as mentioned previously. Unregulated subsidiaries who buy land without planning permission, and then obtain it, are in a position to make enormous windfall profits.

It is suspected that this is already a feature of portfolios being prepared on the assets of the water industry in order to attract big investors, but if this is the case then we are unlikely to be told about it for everything has now been covered by the English blanket of secrecy.

It is very hard indeed to find out anything – even at an official level, even for researchers making legitimate enquiries. And just in case efforts are made to get hold of information by the back door, the employees of Thames Water have been told by their management that water privatisation is a subject which cannot be discussed with anyone – not even family or friends. All outsiders have to be treated as potential investors who might spread price-sensitive information. A letter to Thames Water employees spelled out the position to them in no uncertain terms.

Someone, somewhere is in line to make an awful lot of money out of some of our most beautiful countryside, but not us. That much at least is certain.

16

The Legal Position

At present there are two bodies considering legal action against the government over water privatisation – the European Commission and the Association of Metropolitan Authorities. It would be comforting to think that one or the other or both might succeed but, on present showing, this seems unlikely – although it would certainly not encourage prospective investors.

As has already been emphasised, this country falls far below the standards of the European Directives on water quality. The European Commission is insisting that we clean up our act on nitrates, pesticides, aluminium, lead, coliforms from sewage and PAHS (compounds found in the bitumen linings of water mains) which are believed to be carcinogenic. Some Water Authorities have already admitted that it will be into the next century before they can comply with the Directives.

It seems that the Water Authorities, the government and prospective investors have coasted along believing that somehow or other the EEC Directives and the Commission's efforts to impose them could be ignored. This attitude has been assisted by that of Nicholas Ridley who has taken what might be described as a robust approach to the Directives. He has more or less told the European Commission to mind its own business. In fact the quality of water most definitely *is* the Commission's business and it had already embarked on a series of formal proceedings, asking why Britain has allowed a number of water suppliers to continue supplying water containing unacceptable amounts of nitrates and pesticides. Britain, along with all other EEC countries, is supposed to have agreed to the 1980 Directive (already referred to several times) and met its terms by 1985. However, it did not comply with all its terms nor agree a programme for improvement.

We have already seen that the government has actually invited the Water Authorities to have their pollution standards relaxed in the run-up to privatisation, so that they do not have to ensure that their sewage works are brought up to standard. It appears that that was not all that was offered. Yet another document leaked to Dr John Cunningham appears to allow wide discretion by private water companies in tackling pollution from sources such as iron, lead, nitrates and pesticides. In fact the document appears to exempt nitrate and iron pollution as firm indicators of quality deterioration (according to *The Independent*, 22 December 1988), stating that lead levels in water could be allowed to reach twice the limit laid down by the European Commission and the World Health Organisation guidelines without an automatic requirement for remedial action.

Private suppliers would have broad scope in deciding the terms on which they monitor pesticide pollution of their own waters. They would, it seems, be allowed to 'assess as far as practicable which pesticides are used in significant amounts within the catchment area'. Compulsory monitoring is specified for only two – out of over a thousand – pesticides, Atrazine and Simazine. The regulation on lead lays down a requirement for remedial action only if water concentrations exceed 100 micrograms per litre 'either frequently or to an appreciable extent'. The EEC and WHO level is 50 micrograms.

Even more amazing is what it has to say on iron and nitrate pollution, namely, that as water quality could vary for seasonal or other reasons, concentrations of iron or nitrate in water 'did not in itself necessarily indicate a material deterioration in quality'.

There is no doubt that the government has known exactly what it was doing. In 1988, one of the then European Commissioners, Mr Stanley Clinton Davis, wrote to the government expressing the concern of the EEC over the proposed privatisation legislation. (He and his colleague were later replaced by Mrs Thatcher.) However, the government pressed ahead, presumably hoping that the new environment commissioners might prove more malleable. At first, the EEC protested privately at the reserve government powers built into the Water Bill which would allow it to exempt the new private companies from EEC quality standards. But now the whole question has come out into the open.

In a statement made to *The Independent* (6 February 1989), Mr Clinton Davies confirmed that he had indeed written to the government on the subject of exemptions not approved by Brussels and also challenging plans to allow the privatised companies to monitor their own water supplies. 'I expressed concern on behalf of the Commission about certain aspects of the legislation. It is essential that the legislation and the regulations that flow from it comply with the Commission's water directives.'

By February 1989 the European Commission had made its position clear and public. The quality of British drinking water must comply with its standards before the industry is privatised and any provision in the Water Bill which deferred this would be illegal. This has thrown something of a spanner in the works although the implications appear to have been kept quiet. It would, quite simply, mean that all prospectuses for the sale of the ten Water Authorities would have to include a note of the substantial costs required to meet EEC quality standards. Sr Carlo Ripa di Meana, the European Commissioner for the Environment, stated that the Commission would not bow to British pressure over the issue. Referring to meetings he had had with Department of the Environment officials (*The Guardian*, 8 February 1989), he said: 'We are not willing to allow any member state to try and jump over EEC rules regarding drinking water. No government has the right to give any exemption. This would be illegal.'

The choice in fact is a simple one. If the government decides to defy the EEC regulation it risks condemnation by the European Court. If it puts the full costs into the sale prospectuses it risks losing investors.

Behind the scenes it has made the Water Authorities jittery.

They had been led to believe that there would be no problems over the relaxation of EEC standards and regard this, and the self-monitoring of pollution, as vital to the success of the flotation. A wide range of public relations tactics had been considered to reassure the public over water safety, according to a report in *The Guardian* (9 February 1989) under the front page banner headline 'Euro-crisis Hits Water Sell-off'.

Just what had been proposed came to light only because the various documents were found by Friends of the Earth in a paper recycling plant. This is where an element of farce creeps in. While the idea of spending money on cleaning up water for real appears to be a terrifying one, cleaning up the image is something else entirely, where money would be no object. Among the bright ideas discussed have been sponsorship of a wet T-shirt competition for models in *The Sun*, getting promotional material on to the long-running soap opera *EastEnders* and persuading a TV weather man to drink a glass of water while being televised. Sports personalities like Sharron Davies and Chay Blyth would be used to put over the water quality message. Water, in fact, would become just another commodity to be glossily packaged.

Other information in the documents was more pertinent to current thinking. One document, dated May 1988, spelled out how crucial it was for the EEC standards to be relaxed. 'The industry needs agreement between EC, UK and water authorities on a mode of compliance which is sustainable into and beyond privatisation.' The Department of the Environment is 'taking the lead in this and they *must* (their italics) succeed'. Another document explained that a Lloyds Merchant Bank director, Mr Richard Fortin, had described the water companies as intending 'to fool' the stock market by pressing for flotation in a way which would allow some companies to fetch artificially high prices. Institutional investors would, in any event, be favoured at the expense of small consumers by being offered a 'general share' in all the water firms. Any investor putting up small sums would only be able to buy a share in an individual Water Authority.

Yet another clause said it was essential to pass costs on in full to consumers and to ensure companies have 'satisfactory rights of appeal against regulators'. Discussions were under way on how to handle the PR side of 'non-compliance of sewage treatment with statutory consents'.

However, two quotes in particular are, perhaps, the most revealing. The first, that of passing through the cost of compliance with EC standards to consumers, is 'one of the *very* (their italics) key issues. Without satisfactory cost pass through, the utilities would be hopelessly unattractive.' The second refers to that one reason why water should be privatised before electricity, namely, that 'it is politically less popular and therefore needs to get in early to avoid the danger of being ditched as the electricity floats begin or as the 1991/92 Election gets nearer'.

These documents have been particularly useful since information is in such short supply. For instance, a committee set up by the government to vet all documents on the run-up to privatisation is attempting to block publication of details of drinking water quality and pollution incidents affecting consumers in Yorkshire. This special committee, steered by the government, consists of lawyers and merchant bank advisers. The bulletin in question has been published quarterly for the last fourteen years.

At the present moment, the EC and the government appear to be on a collision course. Not only does the EC insist that our water be brought up to the standards of its current Directives, it is actually planning a new one aimed at futher toughening the controls on nitrate pollution. The new Directive would require Britain to designate 'vulnerable zones' where nitrates pollute drinking water above EC standards of 50 milligrams per litre, covering surface fresh water, ground water, lakes, estuaries and coastal waters and also require compulsory restrictions on chemical fertilisers and animal manure used by farmers. It would also restrict sewage discharges in zones serving over 5,000 people. Britain would be expected to keep annual figures of all nitrogen used in fertilisers and manure and report to the EC every three years.

Behind-the-scenes activity has been frantic and reports began to emerge from those who 'let it be known' that agreement between EC and this country was near. However, this appeared to be an optimistic assessment of the real position. Ironically, choosing Mrs Thatcher's much vaunted Ozone Conference in London, in March 1989, to make his position clear, Sr Carlo Ripa di Meana told Nicholas Ridley that the EC would not grant special exemption to Britain to allow it to relax EC standards on water purity in the run up to privatisation. Mr Ridley had hoped he had made his case with the EC and that it would, in the final analysis, allow the private companies the indefinite period the government wanted to bring water up to EC standards.

At present, it is impossible to know what will happen. There is no doubt that the European Commission could, if it wished, initiate legal proceedings and that this would be a devasting blow to government plans. Whether it will do so remains to be seen. The view of EC officials is that the issue is not about whether or not to privatise – which is a domestic political issue – but that the Commission has an obligation to see that its Directives are complied with. Water standards, they say, are just one of a number of areas with regard to the environment where Britain drags its feet. 'There is increasing concern about our environment and health standards throughout the community,' said a spokesman. 'We cannot be seen to allow national governments to avoid responsibilities for domestic political convenience.'

On 21 April 1989, the EC announced it was giving Britain just two months to produce costed plans for meeting its tough water quality standards and that failure could definitely result in the government being taken to court. Questioned on this Nicholas Ridley said that his estimate that meeting EEC standards could cost up to £24bn may be out of date but he gave no indication of what the new estimates were likely to be. However, he said, the costs would be included on the flotation prospectuses. The EC wants definite target dates by which British water must be brought up to standard and it is most unlikely that it would allow a period of time longer than two years.

In documents accompanying this announcement, it was also shown that the government could have acted before 1985 to meet the nitrate limits in water had it so desired, and that there is now no question of the EC being prepared to wait until the government's preferred date of 1995.

It also appears that consumers are being denied information which would enable them to report Water Authorities to the EEC for breaching drinking water standards because it might put off investors. A comprehensive set of vetting rules was leaked to Friends of the Earth. Correspondence between a Mrs Susan Fletcher, an SLD member of Stockton-on-Tees Council, and Northumbrian Water confirmed that this code was being used to block information, according to *The Guardian* (20 April 1989). She had asked the authority for details of all samples of the water supply which exceeded EEC maximum admissible concentrations in the last twelve months, and was told that in the immediate pre-privatisation period the authority was precluded from releasing the type of information requested 'due to restrictions imposed by the Financial Services Act'.

Meanwhile, the Metropolitan Authorities are proceeding with their plans to sue. On 20 April 1989, it was announced that six of them – Manchester, Liverpool, Sheffield, Hull, Birmingham and Exeter – had appointed a firm of solicitors to contest the sell-off of what they consider to be partly their own assets. Collectively, they say that some £5bn worth of assets, handed over to the water authorities in 1983, are theirs. 'The phoney war,' said a spokesman quoted in *The Independent* (21 April 1989), 'is now over.'

Mr John Humphries, a former board member of Thames Water and a Conservative himself, had told an Association of Metropolitan Authorities Conference, in Sheffield, earlier in the year that a similar challenge through the courts had been prepared in 1986 when privatisation was first mooted. At that time a legal opinion from Mr David Widdicombe, QC, who was advising the Department of the Environment on rating reform, said that the government did not 'own' the Water Authorities. 'If there is any beneficial or equitable ownership it resides in those ratepayers and others who originally contributed the money,' he said. The 1973 Act had not changed the position. The reason the Metropolitan Authorities had not pursued the matter in 1986 was because the government had dropped the bill in the run-up to the general election. He went on to tell the conference that a similar legal challenge to the ownership of the

Trustee Savings Bank through the English and Scottish courts had delayed flotation for eighteen months.

Birmingham City Council puts a preliminary valuation of £507m on its investment between 1853 and 1973 when the city's water assets were merged with those from other local authorities and then the whole lot transferred to Severn Trent Water. 'If the industry is no longer to be publicly controlled then we want our assets back. If, for some technical reason, the government insists we can't physically have them back, we want compensation for them in full.' He continued: 'We believe the government is committing daylight robbery in selling an industry which doesn't belong to it.'

Finally, the Labour Party came out and said that it will take water back into public ownership by any means necessary, however much is sold off by the government. Shadow industry spokesman Brian Gould pointed out that if the government sold off 51 per cent then it would only need to buy back 2 per cent to return it to public control.

How effective can any of this be? At this stage it is just not possible to know. Believable legal action from the Metropolitan Authorities coupled with the threat of it from the European Commission might delay flotation. If there was such a delay then the position could change dramatically in the run-up to the next election for investors would be faced with two challenges – the cost of cleaning up water and the possibility of the government failing to make its case in the courts.

They might ponder John Humphries' view of the basic reason why the government is so desperate to privatise water. 'They want to shift the responsibility for cleaning up water off their backs – it's as simple as that.'

Endpiece

So we are left with the question – why privatise water? There is absolutely no doubt whatsoever that it is deeply unpopular, with three out of four voters being opposed to it. This issue, almost above all others, shows us the state of the democracy about which we prate. A deeply political decision has been forced on an unwilling society by a Prime Minister who, according to Hugo Young's Channel 4 programme on the Thatcher years, has actually described those in her own party in favour of consensus politics as 'quislings', supported by a group of hard right ideologues and those likely to make money out of it. Our 'first past the post' electoral system has allowed an uneven majority in Parliament to push it through regardless of everything – including basic common sense. No matter how many hundreds of thousands or millions of people are opposed to the idea, unless putative legal action by the European Commission and/or the local authorities holds it up water will be privatised by the winter of 1989–90.

It is hard to imagine any other European governments that would go ahead against such opposition, not least because their electoral systems mean they *have* to listen to the views not only of their electorates but of other parties on which they may need to depend for support.

A decent, intelligent government would be looking at the existing situation, its rotting sewers, its substandard sewage works, filthy beaches, polluted water, the possible court cases waiting in the wings and would seriously consider a charter for this most vital of all needs. A useful basis might be provided by the one drawn up by NALGO. It calls for:

- *Public interest to be put before private profit* The needs of the public are simply incompatible with the aims of private enterprise in a service like water. Public ownership is the only way to ensure a responsible approach to providing a high quality water service.

- *Renewal of the nation's infrastructure* Government controls on borrowing to be lifted and the money to be squandered on privatisation invested instead in replacing old and decaying sewers and water mains.
- *Defence of public safety* Flood protection, sea defences and land drainage to be kept properly funded and in public ownership.
- *Environmental protection* This cannot be left to private companies interested only in one thing – making a profit.
- *Public health* There must be proper and responsible application of European Directives on bathing water and drinking water quality. Essential research into water and public health must receive full funding – whether it is immediately 'profitable' or not.
- *Cleaner water* A serious programme is needed to remove toxic substances like lead, nitrates, pesticides and aluminium from the water supply.
- *An end to secrecy* People have a right to know how their water service is run and how the authorities take their decisions. The public must be admitted to Water Authority meetings and all aspects of environmental pollution, effluent discharge, etc. must be openly discussed.
- *More accountability* Communities have a right to have a say in how their service is run and to exercise democratic control through elected representatives.
- *Adequate staffing* Over 13,000 jobs have gone in the water industry and our water has become ever more polluted while services have declined. Proper staffing levels needs to be maintained if a good service is to be provided.
- *A national strategy* The industry needs a co-ordinating body – but one with the power to operate effectively, not an understaffed and underresourced unit like the proposed National Rivers Authority.

Given that that authority will be forced on us with privatisation, Greenpeace, in *Poison on Tap*, provides a long list of recommendations as to how it should operate. It should, for instance, set mandatory deadlines to achieve Grade 2 rivers for present Grade 3 and 4 rivers and these should not be extended by any Secretary of State. It should prosecute more vigorously than its predecessors when pollution offences occur whether these are specific incidents or breaches of consents. A 'polluter must pay' principal must be effectively implemented and charges made for any discharge made directly into a river or estuary.

Courts must view water pollution offences far more seriously, imposing stiffer penalties with the maximum amount increased, and with Crown Court proceedings in the most serious cases. In addition, the relevant section of the existing Act (COPA) regarding the revision of a consent, if it is damaging the river's flora and fauna, should be included in the Water Bill as recommended by the House Select Committee on the Environment but refused by the government. In future, the NRA should abandon any informal policy for granting consents and all powers currently held under COPA should be transferred to the Secretary of State. All consents should be reviewed regularly and more stringent conditions adopted. The current *Red List* of pollutants is inadequate. *All* bioaccumulative chemicals should be banned from the aquatic environment and the new Water Bill should also contain a clause which says that if a company's discharge contains a number of substances, it should not be considered as just one offence but as a separate offence for each individual substance.

With regard to access to information, public registers should be designed in a way which makes them intelligible to the public and all data on them can be used to initiate prosecutions. The 'right to know' should cover all information about which industries discharge into the sewage system together with the nature and quality of the effluent and all monitoring data.

No charges should be made for a member of the public who wishes to discuss general pollution issues with the NRA and charges for consulting the public registers should be absolutely minimal and centrally set. This service must be advertised with applications for consent to discharge.

The NRA should have sufficient resources available, with substantial industrial contributions, to undertake a more comprehensive chemical and biological sampling programme. It should also publish figures annually on levels of compliance of all consents to rivers, estuaries and sewers and this information on river quality should be more widely available. It should issue an annual report on the number of prosecutions, specifying exactly what the offences were and under which sections of the new Water Bill and COPA they were brought.

Industry should disconnect immediately from the sewage system and address the problem of waste by a 'reduction at source' programme, and any sampling being undertaken by the NRA should not be made known to the discharger. Sample results should appear on a register within twenty-eight days of being taken. Companies should be left in no doubt that they will be liable for prosecution if they discharge chemicals not on their consent. All chemical compounds should be characterised in full on consents and the use of the parameter of Chemical Oxygen Demand should be abandoned.

At present, most Water Authorities cooperate in providing biological and chemical survey data on reasonable request from the public, but this is not mandatory. It should be made compulsory. The classification system itself needs to be totally overhauled to take more account of chemical pollution and its impact on the environment. The new Water Bill ought to specify a compulsory sampling regime for the NRA with a fixed minimum number of samples taken from a discharge. It must be given substantial powers to enforce prevention measures on companies in order to minimise pollution incidents, and its board and the Regional Advisory Committees must include adequate representation of conservation, recreational and environmental interests.

The charter presupposes that either water is not privatised or if it is then it will be taken back into public ownership. The recommendations from Greenpeace (which I have précised) allow for the continuation of a National Rivers Authority but as a truly independent body, adequately resourced and with real teeth.

The reality is, however, likely to be far harsher. On the one side, there will be the general public, most of whom do not want their water to be privatised. They will be paying far more for it, there will be no guarantee that its quality will improve (rather the reverse), they will have absolutely no choice if their water is both dear and dirty as they will have nowhere else to go, and they will have no say on how the water supply is administered. They are also likely to find their access to what are now public beauty spots severely restricted or charged for. They are even likely to find their water company is owned by a French multinational which puts the source of power even further away. On the other side, there is a Prime Minister who now has almost absolute power and whose idea this is, her ideologues both inside and outside Westminster, the mindless lobby fodder who will trudge through the lobbies to vote the bill through whatever their private reservations, and those interests likely to make a quick killing out of the sale, most especially the developers. What a prospect!

If nothing else, the privatisation of water has shown just where we are now without any kind of written Constitution, Bill of Rights or Freedom of Information Act.

The situation has not been expressed better than by Tom Paine in *The Rights of Man*. He found it almost beyond belief that the British people not only invited a foreigner (William of Orange) to become their King but that Parliament handed over to the monarchy their submission 'to the end of time', which in effect meant their submission to Parliament. It left us, in reality, without a Constitution. As Paine says: 'A constitution is not a thing in name only, but in fact. It has not an ideal, but a real existence; and wherever it cannot be produced in a visible form, there is none. A constitution is a thing antecedent to a government, and a government is only the creature of a constitution.' It should contain 'the principles on which government should be established, the manner in which it shall be organised, the powers it shall have, the mode of elections, the duration of Parliaments and *the powers which the executive part of the government shall have* (my italics) . . . and the principles on which it should act and by which it should be bound.'

But we have no such deliberated Constitution and therefore

no real rights except that of voting every four or five years. Paine even antedated Freedom of Information Acts, saying, 'the people's enemies take care to represent government as a thing made up of mysteries which only themselves understood; and they hid from the understanding of the nation, the only thing that was beneficial to know, namely that government is nothing more than a national association acting on the principles of society'. He continued his theme in another pamphlet: 'Not withstanding the mystery with which the science of government has been enveloped, for the purpose of enslaving, plundering and imposing upon mankind, it is of all things the least mysterious and most easy to be understood. The meanest capacity cannot be at a loss if it begins its inquiries at the right point.'

Tom Paine and his *Rights of Man* are not irrelevant to the privatisation of water. A clean and available water supply is surely one of the most basic of human rights and is the commodity, above all others, which should not be sold at a profit. Yet our very political system and the way it has evolved over the years now makes this almost a certainty.

We will pay more for our polluted water because of a mixture of political ideology and greed.

JOSEPH CHAMBERLAIN It is difficult and indeed almost impossible to reconcile the rights and interests of the public with the claims of an individual company seeking as its natural and legitimate object the largest private gain.

TOM PAINE ... government is nothing more than a national association acting on the principles of society.

MARGARET THATCHER There is no such thing as society, only individuals.

So she has privatised water.

Select Bibliography of Reports

On Aspects of Pollution

Acid Waters in the UK, by Andrew Tickle (Greenpeace, 1988).
A Critical Overview of Current Waste Disposal Practice (Greenpeace, 1985).
An Investigation of Pesticide Pollution in Drinking Water in England and Wales, by Andrew Lees and Karen McVeigh (Friends of the Earth, 1988).
Pesticide Residues and Food, by Pete Snell and Kirsty Nicol (The London Food Commission, 1988).
Poison in the System, by Tim Birch (Greenpeace, 1989).
The Pollution of the Severn Estuary, by Brian Rice (Greenpeace, 1986).
The Golden List of British Beaches, from The Marine Conservation Society, 1988–9.
The Public Health Implications of Sewage Pollution of Bathing Water (The Robens Institute of Industrial and Environmental Health and Safety, 1988).
The Thames Estuary – A Status Report (Greenpeace, 1986).
Toxic Waste, Report of House of Commons Select Committee on the Environment (HMSO, 1989).

European Commission

European Parliament Session Documents 1987–8 (Document A2-0298/87 English Edition).
The Implementation of European Community Legislation Relating to Water: A Threat to Privatisation?, by Ken Collins MEP and David J. Earnshaw (Leeds University, 1988).

Politics

Environment in Trust (Department of Environment, 1989).
Water Down the Drain (NALGO for Joint Trade Union Water Anti-Privatisation Campaign, 1988).
The Water Bill – Key Issues (NALGO 1988).
Hansard 7 December 1988 – Second Reading of Water Bill.
Hansard 6 February 1989 – Guillotine Debate on Water Bill.

Hansard, Standing Committee on Water Bill. Proceedings for 26, 31 January 1989, 2, 7, 9, 14 February 1989.

General

Liquid Assets – The Likely Effects of Privatisation of Water Authorities on Wildlife Habitats and Landscape, by John Bowers, Kathy O'Donnell and Sarah Whatmore (Leeds University for CPRE, 1988).

Privatisation of the Water Industry: Some Outstanding Issues, by Bowers, O'Donnell and S.G. Ogden (Leeds University, 1988).

Research Note: Water Privatisation and the Water Bill, by Caroline Gilmour and Priscilla Baines (House of Commons Library Research Division, 1988).

The Financial Implications of the Privatisation of the Water Supply and Sewerage Services – A Current Assessment, from Arthur Collins & Co., Advisers on Finance of Public Authorities in the UK and Abroad (1988).

Water Down the Drain (Joint Action for Water Services, 1988).

Report on NALGO's Delegation to the French Water Industry, October 1988 (NALGO 1988).

Index